Paul Erdman's Money Book

Paul Erdman's Money Book

An Investor's Guide
to Economics and
Finance

Paul Erdman

RANDOM HOUSE   NEW YORK

Grateful acknowledgment is made to the following for permission to reprint previously published material:

Academic Press, Inc.: Excerpts from the *Cambridge Journal of Economics*, September 1978.
Copyright: Academic Press Inc. (London) Ltd. Used with permission.

Aden Analysis: Excerpt from Volume 2, No. IV, April 10, 1983. Copyright © 1983 by Aden Analysis,
4425 West Napoleon Avenue, Metairie, LA. Used with permission.

Anglo American Corporation of South Africa Limited: Graph from *The Future World Price of Gold*,
by Horace Brock, 1981. Reproduced by permission of the editor of *Optima*, published by Anglo
American Corporation of South Africa Limited.

Associated Press: Table—"Interest Rates: The Ones to Watch," appearing in the *San Francisco
Chronicle*, Wednesday, November 2, 1983. Copyright © 1983 by Associated Press. Used with permission.

Dow Jones & Company, Inc.: Excerpt from "Talking Money with Milton Friedman," by Peter Brimelow,
October 25, 1982, p. 7. Reprinted by permission of *Barron's*. Copyright © 1982 by Dow Jones & Company,
Inc. Excerpts from "Private Borrowing and the Federal Deficit," February 3, 1983, by Evan Galbraith;
"International Bankers Take Steps to Restore Faith in Their System," by Art Pine, September 15, 1982; "Bad
News Has Little Effect on Gold's Price," by Roger Lowenstein, December 21, 1981; and "Powerless Feeling:
Utilities Face a Crisis Over Nuclear Plants—Costs, Delays Mount," by Geraldine Brooks, Ron Winslow and
Bill Richards, December 1, 1983. All four reprinted by permission of *The Wall Street Journal*. All copyright
© Dow Jones & Company, Inc. All Rights Reserved.

The Economist: Excerpt from "Now Thrive Popeye," *The Economist*, January 29, 1983, p. 11.
Used with permission.

Fortune Magazine Art Department: Graph from "Is Inflation Coming Back?," by A. F. Ehrbar,
Fortune, March 21, 1983, p. 63. Copyright © 1983 Time, Inc. All rights reserved. Used with permission.

Hambrecht & Quist, Inc.: Graph from 1983 Technology Index, copyright © 1984 by Hambrecht & Quist
Incorporated. Used with permission.

Institute for International Economics and M.I.T. Press: Table from *International Debt and the Stability of the
World Economy*, by William Cline. Copyright © 1983 by the Institute for International Economics. All
rights reserved. Distributed by M.I.T. Press, Cambridge, Massachusetts, and London, England. Used with
permission.

International Money Line: Graph from "London Gold P. M. Fix," *International Money Line*,
March 7, 1983, p. 3. Used with permission.

Le Monde: Excerpt from "What Weapons Against War?," by André Fontaine, appearing in
Le Monde, June 18, 1983, p. 12. Used with permission.

W. W. Norton & Company, Inc.: Adaptation of graph from *Principles of Macroeconomics*, Second Edition,
by Edwin Mansfield, Norton, 1977, pp. 362–365. Used with permission.

Peter G. Peterson: Excerpts from "Social Security: The Coming Crash," *The New York Review of Books*,
December 2, 1982, p. 34. Used with permission.

Random House, Inc.: Adaptation of graph from *Dangerous Currents* by Lester Thurow. Copyright © 1983 by
Lester C. Thurow, Inc. Used with permission.

Rutgers University Press: Graph from "Interest Rates Through U.S. History," from *A History of Interest
Rates* by Sidney Homer. Copyright © 1963, 1967 by Rutgers, The State University. Used with permission.

Library of Congress Cataloging in Publication Data

Erdman, Paul, 1932–
Paul Erdman's Money book.

Includes index.
1. United States—Economic conditions—1981–
2. Economics. 3. Finance, Personal. I. Title. II. Title:
Money book.
HC106.8.E72   1984   332.6'78   82–40120
ISBN 0-394-52482-9

Manufactured in the United States of America

24689753

FIRST EDITION

for Constance and Jennifer

PREFACE

Books on economics and finance tend to reflect the immediate environment in which they were written. Thus in the 1970's, when inflation was rising toward double digits, we had a plethora of doom-and-gloom books which, inevitably, concluded by suggesting that we head for either the hills or Switzerland, gun and gold in hand.

Today, reflecting an environment in which we are enjoying both a strong economic recovery and extraordinarily low rates of inflation, we have been getting a plethora of onward-and-upward books which, inevitably, end with the Dow Jones Industrial Average at 3,000 and America once again triumphant.

I have tried to avoid both extremes. Although by nature I am probably an optimist, I think by training I am also a realist. My background in economics tells me that despite the current recovery and low rates of inflation, our nation—in fact our world—is far from solving some very serious and deep-seated problems. To name just two: the $750 billion debt owed our banks by the lesser-developed world; and the enormous deficits being amassed by the non-Communist world, more than $200 billion by the United States and more than $400 billion by the remaining countries. How are we going to finance these deficits and these debts if they continue to grow ever larger? If we fail to get these problems under control, at some point they will overwhelm our system and combine to create credit crunches, banking crises, the revival of inflation, the return of deep recession.

Or will they?

Is it possible that the 1980's will be different? Is it possible that we are in a new era—one in which growth will once again prove sustainable, in which the application of electronics and genetic engineering to our society will revive the industrialized world? Are the 1980's perhaps the decade in which the United States will once again be globally preeminent because the United States is the country that has led the way in the technological development and the financing of these sunrise industries? As a result of this renewed growth, and as a result of America's new strength and confidence, will it be possible, if not to solve, at least to postpone . . . and postpone . . . and postpone . . . the problems I have mentioned until, perhaps, they just go away?

The future no doubt lies somewhere between these two points of view. As you read the initial part of this book you will probably find yourself increasingly disturbed, because it is in that first part that I dwell on the deficit and debt problems and their possible economic and financial consequences. But as the exploration process continues in the rest of the book, you will, I hope, note that I become increasingly optimistic. Believe me, the end is *not* near.

As Casey Stengel said, the game is not over until the game is over. Well, our capitalistic game, our money game, is far from over. It is still the only economic system that works and works well for most of the citizens who are able to participate in it. Sometimes the system malfunctions, and we —all of us—suffer. This will be as true of capitalism in the future as it has been in the past. Thus this "futuristic" book is full of downs—and then ups. But although I have tried to provide a strong dose of reality, I hope that when you have finished it you will agree that if this book has a bias, that bias is on the whole an optimistic one.

ACKNOWLEDGMENTS

I would like to express my thanks to Tom Rosenthal of Secker & Warburg in London for first suggesting and then sponsoring this book.

I am especially indebted to Jason Epstein of Random House in New York. If this book has elements of "quality," they are due to the high standards he sets as an editor and the excellent advice he renders as a scholar.

CONTENTS

Part I

○◎○○◎○○◎○○◎○○◎○○◎○

Where We Are
and How We
Got Here

Chapter 1

o◯oo◯oo◯o

What This Book
Is All About

A T THE END OF JULY 1982 the stock market in New York was at a two-year low, and the bond market was in such bad shape that long-term government bonds were yielding well over 13 percent. Conditions were similar in financial markets from Tokyo to London to Zurich.

Then on August 20, 1982, at a meeting at the Federal Reserve Bank of New York, Mexico's finance minister told more than a hundred bankers that his country couldn't repay its loans. Nor was Mexico the only debtor nation in such difficulties. The international debt crisis had begun. One would have thought that all financial markets, except gold, would as a result go from bad to worse.

They didn't. Instead, what followed was one of the greatest stock and bond market rallies in history. Between August 1982 and June 1983 the Dow Jones Industrial Average went from 777 to over 1,200; the Tokyo market rose 22 percent; the London stock market rose 30 percent; the Swiss gained 33 percent, the Dutch 64 percent, the Canadian 75 percent, the Swedish 125 percent. During that same period dollar-denominated bonds provided a return of 38 percent on average.

Why?

Answer: interest rates. As dollar interest rates began to ratchet down from the absurd highs they had reached in that summer of '82, the market —no, *markets* around the world—began to ratchet up. Subsequently every 1 percent decrease in interest rates produced a 50–75 point increase in the Dow. But what did that bankers' meeting with Mexico's finance minister have to do with interest rates?

Everything. Because it was those hundred American bankers who, after hearing what their Mexican visitor had to say, gave the final warning to the Federal Reserve: unless it eased up radically on money conditions, thereby providing the banking system with considerably more liquidity, there would be no way that the banks in New York and Chicago and California could refinance Mexico without creating global monetary havoc. If Mexico could not be refinanced, it would go into default. If Mexico went into default, probably dozens of other debtor nations in the Third World would follow. Since collectively these debtors in the so-called lesser-developed countries owed the banking system of the industrialized world over $700 billion, such a chain of defaults might well collapse the international banking system. The Crash of '82 would be upon us.

The Fed caved in, pushed money into the system and gave the banks the liquidity they needed. The debt crisis was gradually—and temporarily —brought under control. But another result of those falling interest rates in the United States was an economic recovery which produced those bull markets. A side effect was that the value of stocks and bonds in investors' hands around the world increased by at least one trillion dollars in the year that followed.

To go back to square one, the link between those profits and the Mexican debt crisis was *interest rates*. In this book we are going to be devoting a lot of attention to that pivotal link in our economic/financial system. And as we move from the present to the future, we are going to try to spot the next potential "Mexico" that could radically affect the direction that interest rates will take in 1985 and 1986 and once again fundamentally affect the value of our investments . . . perhaps next time in the opposite direction.

On February 22, 1983, the price of crude oil on the spot (cash) market in Rotterdam collapsed to below $29 a barrel. In the week that followed, the gold price plummeted by more than $100 an ounce, bottoming out on February 28 at $400. Why? This time the link between the economic event and the investment result was *inflation*, or, more accurately, *inflationary expectations*. Since 1973 the price of oil had moved inexorably upward. The tenfold increase in oil prices in ten years had been primarily responsible for the greatest bout of inflation the world had seen in this century. Energy costs have a key, pervasive influence on all prices. When oil hit $40 a barrel, almost every energy expert on earth was predicting that the next stop was $60, then $80, and probably $100 by the end of the decade. Inflation was, therefore, destined to become a permanent part of our lives. On February 22, 1983, all such expectations were suddenly turned upside down: with oil at $29 a barrel and falling, instead of $40 a barrel and rising, the outlook for the future rate of inflation was radically altered. Future inflation would probably be closer to 4 percent than to 10 percent.

Gold lives or dies by inflation. It is the classic hedge against the loss of purchasing power of paper money. Kill inflation, and the gold-bugs crawl back into the woodwork. That's what happened in late February 1983. But now the question is: how much longer will inflation remain under control? When it revives, won't the gold price go right back up again? For the answer, read on.

In July 1983 the bull markets in financial assets (stocks and bonds) stalled. The reason? Excessive money supply growth. Americans have turned into a nation of M1 watchers. When M1, the "hot" transactional money in our system composed of cash and private checking accounts, grows too rapidly over an extended period of time, history tells us that eighteen to twenty-four months later, inflation almost always starts to rise, as do interest rates. In the twelve months preceding July 1983, M1 had grown almost 14 percent—a rate unprecedented in recent times. In the summer of '83 the market participants began increasingly to feel that these monetary chickens were going to come home to roost—and ruin the low-inflation/high-growth atmosphere which had been so conducive to the bull markets that had begun a year earlier in both stocks and bonds. For if the Fed now suddenly stopped monetary growth, a credit crunch would result, interest rates would soar and the end result could be recession, which would ruin the markets. If the Fed did not change its policy and kept pouring money into the system, the result would certainly be inflation and soaring interest rates down the line and, again, recession, which would ruin the markets. An increasing number of investors therefore felt they faced a no-win situation. Thus the markets stalled.

So here we have the third key phenomenon that must be constantly watched—and its future path assessed—since what happens to the *money supply* will basically affect the future rates of both *inflation* and *interest*, and all three together will basically determine the investment climate and thus the future price of your IBM stock, your AT&T bonds and your house. I will try to assess which policies the Federal Reserve will follow in the future in regard to money supply. As it turned out, the 1983 "monetary scare" was premature: the Fed was able to temporarily throttle back monetary growth in the second half of 1983 without creating any major economic problems. However, despite that calming respite, I can tell you right now that I am not terribly sanguine about this aspect of our future. With deficits in the United States seemingly stuck at $200 billion, and with deficits in the rest of the world now totaling twice that amount, it is very difficult to see how they can be financed unless governments create an awful lot of new money during the rest of the 1980's.

The fourth, and final, basic economic variable that is key to our economic future, and the future of the assets in which we have invested our money, is *growth*. With enough future growth, the wealth that we create will prove more than sufficient to pay for entitlement benefits to the old and the needy, weapons galore for the Pentagon and endless bailouts of the debtors of the Third World. Those deficits would gradually, but surely, disappear. The Dow might end up hitting 2,000. But if growth stops—if another major, prolonged recession hits us in the 1980's—what then? Will the Social Security system run out of money? Will the Third World debt situation suddenly turn ugly, and once again pose a threat to the entire banking system? Will the price of gold then skyrocket, while the stock markets of the world collapse?

In my novels I have always set the stories in the future. The "plot" in this book is similarly set in the future, in fact in the immediate future. It is predicated on the thesis that we will soon be at another crossroads, and that two alternative paths will lie before us: a "high road," which will bring us sustained economic growth and low inflation and will allow us to avoid both the debt and deficit crises; and a "low road," which will ultimately end in growing economic disintegration.

Then, drawing on my own conclusions as to which road those four key economic variables—money supply, inflation, interest rates and growth— are going to take us along, I will make definitive suggestions as to where you should be investing your money now and where you should be planning to invest it two or three years from now.

Along the way, you are going to get a small dose of the history of economic thought—of what John Maynard Keynes really said, what supply-side economics and Milton Friedman and Arthur Laffer are all about. For it is these men and their theories which have provided the intellectual tools that the politicians and bankers and entrepreneurs have used, often unknowingly, to create the economic situation—perhaps a better word is mess—in which we find ourselves and from which we may, or may not, be emerging today. On top of that, you are also going to get a very small dose of economic history as we try to determine where we are now by examining how we got here in the first place.

In the end I hope that you will feel qualified to take over from there —to act as your own economist, to make your own projections and to formulate from them your own investment strategies.

Chapter 2

o◯ooo◯oo◯o

Where We Are and How
We Got Here

THE DECADE OF THE 1980's is obviously a product of the previous three and a half decades since the end of World War II—and to go even farther back, of the Great Depression of the 1930's. In fact, in many ways it is more a product of the latter than of the former. This is because of a man who has probably had more to do with our present income and wealth, but also our fear that we might lose it, than anybody else in this century. His name was John Maynard Keynes (Lord Keynes, as he was known after being raised to the peerage in his later years). He died before even half of this century was over—in 1946, to be exact—but his theories live on in the form of deficit spending, the International Monetary Fund and even in the words of Richard Nixon, who, in 1971, muttered the seemingly unutterable statement, at least for a Republican, that he was a Keynesian.

Who exactly was Keynes? To begin with, he epitomized what, I guess, some Americans would term "an effete Englishman." He was a member of the Bloomsbury group of intellectuals and a friend of the writer Virginia Woolf; a Cambridge man, married to the famous ballerina Lydia Lopokova and a homosexual. But despite such appearances he was one of the most brilliant and productive men of our century—in the judgment of many, the Albert Einstein of the social sciences. Yet, especially in the United States, and more especially among those Americans to the right of center, he is vilified as the architect of all that is evil, or in any case all that has gone wrong in recent years, in our economic system.

The new prophets—the new, or perhaps, as we shall see, the *renewed*, gurus of economics—are Milton Friedman, the man upon whom England's prime minister Margaret Thatcher built her political future; Arthur Laffer, upon whom Ronald Reagan has bet his; and Friedrich von Hayek, an obscure economist of Austrian origin who has emerged as the patron saint of the libertarian, i.e., free market, school of economic thought. Hayek's elevation to the hierarchy of modern economists was confirmed when, to the satisfaction of the advocates of supply-side economics, he received the Nobel Prize in economics in 1974, an honor otherwise reserved almost exclusively for Keynesians such as Paul Samuelson of MIT or James Tobin of Yale, respectively among the first and the most recent to have received this honor. But no doubt most important is the fact that this "anti-Keynesian" school of economic thought has risen to primacy through the ascendancy of one of its disciples to the presidency of the United States, of another to the office of prime minister of Great Britain, and by the return to power in West Germany of a right-wing coalition of the same "reactionary" persuasion.

How do they differ? Why was Keynes the architect of our past, and why are Friedman, Laffer and Hayek the architects of our present? And who is going to be the architect of our future?

Let's start with Keynes and the past.

Until the 1930's the "science" of economics was dominated by what was thought to be a basic, immutable law of nature: supply creates its own demand. It was logical. You make something (say a pair of shoes), you get paid for it and now you use that money to buy something of equivalent value from somebody else (say food from a farmer). Supply created and also equaled demand. Right? For a century and a half everybody thought so—with the exception of a few crackpots like Karl Marx.

To be sure, even noncrackpots in the nineteenth and early twentieth centuries could not help but observe that at times this "law" seemed to be temporarily suspended. There were constantly recurring economic crises and financial crashes when an "oversupply" appeared to develop. The result was that companies and whole industries would founder because they couldn't sell what they had made. But such crises never lasted very long. Usually within a matter of months, such "oversupply" would disappear as the people who had lost their jobs in bankrupt companies found new jobs in new enterprises producing new products, and with their incomes restored as they once again got paid for contributing to the "supply" of new products, they would start buying. This renewed demand would sop up the "oversupply" that had been hanging over the market —and *voilà*, order, balance, equilibrium and thus full employment for anybody who wanted to work. According to the theory current at the time, such equilibrium *had* to return. Say's law said so: supply always creates its own demand. And although Jean Baptiste Say, who decreed this law, was a Frenchman, his formulation summarized the core teaching of the Scot who was the father of classical economics, Adam Smith.

All of this seemed to make sense, more or less, until the crash of 1929, after which a situation developed that had no precedent, one whose explanation you could seek in vain in the writings of any of the classical economists from Adam Smith through his great successors—Ricardo, Hobson, Marshall. It was a depression in which such an oversupply developed that farmers burned their crops and abandoned their land; tens of thousands of factories stopped production, never to start again; in the United States alone, ten thousand banks closed and never reopened; 10 percent, then 15 percent, then 20 percent of the labor force was out of work. It started in earnest in 1931, and as the years went by, the crises seemed to deepen. What's more, it was worldwide: the same malaise in Britain, in Germany, in Switzerland. It seemed as if nobody could sell anything to anybody. Where, you might ask, was Say when we needed him?

Enter John Maynard Keynes. In 1936 he published a book under the title *The General Theory of Employment, Interest and Money*. He began by saying in essence that Say had been dead wrong, that classical economics was all wet. Supply did *not* necessarily create an equal amount of demand. Just because someone made something, it didn't necessarily follow that someone would buy it. Equilibrium, therefore, did *not* return once the system went out of whack. Mass unemployment would *not* necessarily go away if we simply relied on "the system" to make it do so. Because, Keynes said, pointing out what was now obvious, the system had broken down. There simply was not enough *demand* to create jobs for everybody who wanted to work: the result was an appalling shortfall in jobs in his country, in the United States, throughout Europe, a shortfall of such magnitude that the very social fabric of the capitalistic world was at stake.

If the problem was inadequate *demand*, and if the "supply side" (to borrow a phrase from the 1980's) did not itself produce such demand, what were we going to do about it?

Artificially stimulate demand, said Keynes. But who could do this and how could it be done? The answer to the "who" was government; the answer to the "how" was deficit spending. The government was going to spend more money than it took in—go into the red—and distribute the money by one means or another to the people so that they could, in effect, buy themselves out of the Depression. The theory was that by the time the economy recovered, the government could easily repay what it had borrowed to set things in motion again.

The need for the artificial stimulation of demand by government arose from the fact, Keynes pointed out, that people did not automatically and fully spend their incomes. The fellow who got paid for making that pair of shoes did not take the fully equivalent amount and buy food with it so that the farmer could, in turn, go out and buy a couple of cans of chewing tobacco and thus keep things humming all down the line. For not only was everyone scared by the current economic situation, but people were even more fearful of the future. They expected things to get worse, and so they opted for liquidity. They began to save an inordinate amount of their incomes.

In normal times such savings could only have been regarded as good and healthy for national economies. The savings went to a bank; the bank lent to Ford Motor Company; Ford built a new car assembly plant in St. Louis and hired five thousand new employees to man it, all of whom now started to buy shoes and food and chewing tobacco and, of course, cars.

All fine and good, theoretically, except that now, because of the gloom that pervaded America after the crash of '29, the people at Ford Motor Company had decided to pull in their horns on a corporate level just as the shoemaker and the farmer had decided to do on an individual level: there would be no new investments until the huge inventory of unsold cars was greatly reduced, and Ford didn't care if the bank offered to lend money at 3 percent for ten years. This was a time for prudent consolidation, not risk-taking.

Thus the whole "automatic" savings-investment-output-income-savings cycle broke down. That "invisible hand" which Adam Smith had invented at the end of the eighteenth century in his classic book *The Wealth of Nations*, that "natural" force which propelled the engine of capitalism, a force generated by the inherent self-interest of human beings, ceased to operate.

If today the problems of the 1930's sound all too familiar, what about the "new" solutions being offered? Do the theories and suggestions of Milton Friedman or Arthur Laffer or Friedrich von Hayek differ basically from those of Say and Smith? Are we not again being told that all we need are tax cuts, which will lead to higher savings, leading automatically and quickly to renewed investment and thus renewed output and thus increased incomes and thus higher tax receipts and thus a balanced budget and thus a return to good times for all? What these men have been telling us is that all we have to do is unleash the private sector by getting government off its back, and it will surely do its thing.

Well, as I write, taxes are down and savings are up and recovery is well under way. But how long will this process last *this* time? And *then* what will happen? Fear about the future continues to abound, and as in the 1930's, such fearful expectations have led first to a massive flight into liquidity—into money market funds—and then to an equally massive flight into "quality," i.e., investments in Treasury bills, notes and bonds by people who had never bought government paper before in their lives. The most recent movement of savings from money market funds to governmentally insured money market accounts at banks—involving well over a third of a trillion dollars in a matter of months—reflects how highly developed this yearning for both liquidity and quality is today. But there is still no significant movement of savings into real investments. For you can't push a string. You can't *force* Ford Motor Company to borrow to build new capacity. And today, under pressure from Japanese competition, Ford Motor Company is back on the defensive: it's not trying to grow, to build new plants, to hire new workers, to conquer new markets. It's just trying to hang on to what it's got!

So maybe what we need today is not a revival of historically suspect supply-side theories but rather a revival of Keynes. After all, he got us out of the last fix. Right? Well, not exactly. Mythology would have it that Franklin Roosevelt met John Maynard Keynes, asked Keynes to explain his theories to him, and from this revelation on the road to Damascus was born the New Deal with its government spending programs that saved the Republic. This is pure baloney. It was World War II and the need for massive rearmament that got the factories going again and got us out of the Depression. Ford, indeed, finally started to tap savings, and tap them massively, to build new assembly plants, but these plants were for making not cars but tanks and aircraft engines and troop carriers. The threat of war and not the theories of Keynes created the demand that had so long been missing, restarting the process that led once more to the "normal" functioning of capitalism.

If there was a country in which Keynesian-like theories were applied in the 1930's, it was Germany. As I found out much to my surprise during my studies at the University of Basel in the mid-1950's, a trio of German economists—Joseph Schumpeter, Arthur Spiethoff and especially Albert Hahn, a banker and economist from Frankfurt am Main—had developed ideas very similar to those of Keynes in the late 1920's and early 1930's. At the time nobody in the Anglo-Saxon world had even heard of these three men, since nobody thought it worthwhile to read anything produced by economists not in residence at either Harvard or Cambridge and writing in any language but English. But Dr. Hjalmar Schacht, whom Hitler had taken on as his first financial adviser following his assumption of power in Germany, had paid attention to these professors, and it was he who first took the "Keynesian" approach on a large scale, using expansionary monetary and fiscal policies to finance public works, especially the building of thousands of kilometers of *Autobahnen* to get things going again in Germany. Things did get going again, but slowly. When Hitler proceeded with his plan for rearmament and then war, which *really* worked, Schacht quit. What worked for Hitler and Germany also worked for Tojo and Japan. Likewise for Churchill and Britain.

The real dawn of Keynes-inspired public policy in the United States came in 1946, when Roosevelt's successor, Harry Truman, signed the Employment Act. This landmark legislation grew out of fear of a huge postwar recession, since, historically, recessions almost inevitably followed peace. Why? For the same reason that war solves depression, but in reverse. When the "artificial stimulus" of government spending on their war machines collapses, the result is an enormous demand gap. Soon all economic activity goes into a deep stall, and everything is back to prewar conditions. It was just such a prospect of a return to the terrible situation of the 1930's that led Truman and Congress to pass this new law of the land, which demanded that should the worst happen in a world now at peace, it was the *responsibility* of the United States government to intervene so as to restore that supply/demand/full employment equilibrium of Monsieur Say. Paradoxically, it is by way of Keynes that we got back to Say and Adam Smith.

During the early postwar years the government pursued such policies and they worked admirably. They worked admirably because the theory was applied in both directions where aggregate demand was concerned. What this means is that when demand was getting out of hand, when too much money was chasing too few goods and forcing prices up instead of increasing output, the government intervened just as it had in the 1930's when there was too little money in the system, but this time it took money *out* of the system by running *surpluses* rather than deficits. The Eisenhower years provided an almost perfect example of how the ebb and flow of government fiscal intervention can produce a tranquil and benign economic environment. The 1950's were almost evenly divided between years of budgetary deficits and budgetary surpluses. Output rose steadily; prices did not.

But then came the 1960's and Vietnam and the Great Society. Ebb and flow no longer alternated as they had in the past. There was now only flow, which is to say, only *deficits*. There was no way that the government could pay for both that war and the new social programs it also wanted without raising taxes to levels that would have strangled the economy and infuriated the voters. And so began the deliberate, insidious, self-destructive misuse of what Keynes had taught. Put crudely, the new attitude was that if some deficit spending was good, more was better. The corollary of this was the attitude that it didn't matter if the national debt began to grow to staggering proportions as a result. After all, Professor Samuelson told us in his textbook, which millions upon millions of students used as their economic bible in the 1960's and 1970's: Don't worry if we are in debt; we owe it to ourselves. What's more, a growing economy will easily "collateralize"—so to speak—a growing debt.

So as of 1984, during the past twenty-three out of twenty-four years the United States has run deficits—has spent more than it took in. And for most of this period the Keynesian medicine continued to work. Demand stimulation by government produced ever-rising output by the private sector. The world enjoyed the greatest increase in the prosperity of its residents since the beginning of time.

That era has now ended.

The medicine no longer works. Demand no longer forever evokes supply any more than supply was forever able to evoke demand. All that government deficits now produce are ever-higher government borrowings and wildly fluctuating interest rates. Such government borrowings are already so high that they eat up all the savings that Americans can generate. In fact, with current annual savings of the entire developed world at $500 billion, the United States government alone must tap at least 40 percent of that to cover the gap between what it takes in each year in taxes and what it gives out for social programs, interest and defense. With Canada, West Germany, France and even Japan running proportionately huge deficits at the same time, and with the Third World relying upon *us* to rescue *it* by granting more and more credit, the global situation seems to be slipping out of control.

If despite the largest deficit spending in the history of the universe—which is as good a description as any of Reagan's supply-side policies and the vast deficit that resulted—the American economy, while recovering robustly, still leaves almost ten million Americans out of work; if the same holds true for the Canadians and the Germans and the French and the

Scandinavians, what will get us and thus the world moving back to full employment and prosperity for all?

Have we reached a point now where both Say *and* Keynes are dead?

If so, where lies salvation?

If nobody knows, is it then inevitable that the system is going to blow up for sure this time?

If not now, then when?

Read on and find out. A hint: the end may be nearing, but it's not here yet.

Chapter 3

o◯oo◯oo◯o

The Cyclical Nature
of Capitalism

I HAVE SUGGESTED that something has gone basically wrong in our system: that we no longer seem to rebound "automatically" to a state of equilibrium where supply and demand are equal, everyone is employed and prices are stable. Instead we lurch from inflation to unemployment, from boom to bust, maybe next time or the time after to the big bust, and after that, who knows?

But hold on, anybody with even a short memory will say: we've *always* gone through such oscillations. Our world is not static; it's dynamic. Everything is always on the move.

True. And, moreover, such movement is always *cyclical.* What's more, we now know that the path of such cycles is, or at least was, *predictable.* Thus those famous "leading economic indicators" that the government issues each month and that are supposed to forecast the cyclical ups and downs.

When a group of economic variables, such as building permits and the money supply, begins to move down in a sustained fashion (for three months in a row), these so-called leading indicators tell us that soon, probably within six months, the whole economy is headed for a recession. (The accuracy of such predictions, however, varies wildly, and in recent history it has taken as long as twenty-three months before the predicted recession actually began.) The leading indicators work better as predictors in the other direction, when the lag between the time the indicators turn up and the revival of the economy is consistently in the one-to-six-month range.

But why this cyclical behavior in the first place?

The pig cycle explains it best. (See Figure 1.) When the price of pork starts to rise, the farmers inevitably expand their operations to breed more pigs. Who wouldn't? Eighteen months later the little pigs that resulted are now big pigs: the supply of pork dramatically increases. The consequent excess supply results in falling prices. Prices fall so far that it costs the farmer more to feed the pigs than he's getting for them in the marketplace. So he stops breeding them. Eighteen months later there is a shortage of pigs. So pork prices start to rise again. Soon such prices exceed feed costs per pig. So on and on.

FIGURE 1
The Pig Cycle

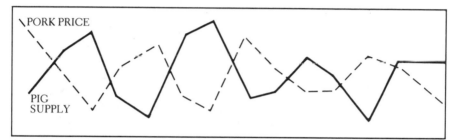

The same process occurs where housing is concerned. But since the "gestation" period for houses is much longer than for pigs, the cycle too is much longer—seven years instead of eighteen months. Or take ships: since it takes even longer to build ships once high freight prices have provided the incentive for shipping lines or oil companies to order them, the shipbuilding cycle is twelve years. But the principle is always the same.

"The" business cycle, then, is the cumulative result of the combined effects of many of these underlying cycles—from short to long, from pigs to ships. It was Clement Juglar, a Frenchman, who, in 1860, "discovered" that such generalized business cycles occurred not only in his own country but also in both Britain and the United States, and deduced that they were intrinsic to capitalism. He further deduced that the time it took for the overall economy to move from prosperity to depression and back to prosperity averaged eight to ten years.

In 1926 a Russian named Nicolai Kondratieff wrote an essay called "The Long Waves of the Business Cycle." He had discovered that in addition to the Juglar cycle, there seemed to be statistical evidence of much longer cycles which spanned not years but decades. He pointed out that a general upswing in the system had begun in 1850 and lasted until 1874; that it was followed by a downswing which had begun in 1875 and continued to 1895, and was then succeeded in turn by the next return to prosperity, which began in 1896 and lasted until 1913.

To fill out the picture, in 1923 two Americans, W. L. Crum and Joseph Kitchin, discovered the shortest cycle of all—just forty months—which seemed to recur with almost absolute regularity in both the United States and England, a movement which they tracked by observing the rise and fall of interest rates, wholesale prices, the volume of bank clearings, and especially inventories.

Figure 2 puts all these cycles together.

FIGURE 2
The Business Cycles

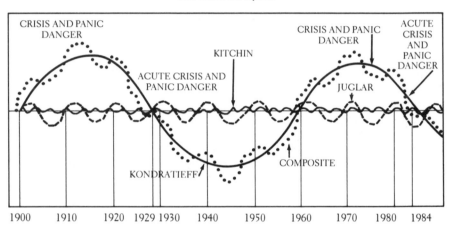

It is the short cycle, the inventory cycle—the forty-month Kitchin cycle —that most of us have grown used to in our lifetime. It is that cycle which both the government and the press track very carefully.

During the thirty-five years since the end of the post–World War II boom we have experienced eight recessions in the United States. Truman gave us one, a mild one, in 1949. Under Eisenhower we had three: a rather serious one which began soon after he took office in 1953, a medium one in 1957 and a mild one in 1960. During the rest of the 1960's we were spared recession. In fact, it was during that decade that American economists had pretty well convinced themselves that they had brought us to the point where they could now "fine-tune" the business cycle out of existence. They believed, and so did a lot of others, that since continuous ever-growing prosperity was now a permanent phenomenon in the United States and probably in the entire Western world as well, the only remaining serious economic challenge that faced us was to achieve a "fair" allocation of this affluence.

Today it is hard to believe that such economic theories prevailed only a dozen years ago. Unfortunately it is with the legacy of such fallacious thinking—the so-called entitlement programs, about which more in a moment—that we must now attempt to live. For what happened was that no sooner had Johnson's programs to achieve massive redistribution of wealth and thus a Great Society really gotten under way than along came that critical year of 1973 and the return of the business cycle in a peculiarly vicious form.

First the oil embargo brought home the fact that America was vulnerable where energy was concerned, so much so that a shah and a few sheiks could bring the most powerful nation on earth almost to its knees within months. Then at the end of 1973 came a recession that proved that the fine-tuning economists had been wrong all along; that our economy was vulnerable both from within and from without; that the onward-and-upward-forever theory was baloney. America's output and income fell back a staggering 9 percent between the end of 1973 and mid-1975; unemployment doubled to almost 9 percent within a year.

By 1973 the brief period in which Americans could believe that they had, once and for all, found the secret to permanent prosperity for themselves, and half of the world as well, was already over. So it was back to business as usual, back to the same old forty months of down and then up and then down again . . . but always a net movement of more up than down. Or so one thought. Unfortunately, that's not the way it turned out.

All of a sudden, or perhaps not so suddenly, we found ourselves in strange new territory. In 1976, three years after the setback of 1973, output actually did turn up, but this time only sluggishly. What was worse, along with the recovery came something new—a rate of inflation that had begun to rise at a speed and to a level that was unprecedented in the United States in this century. But why? After all, Jimmy Carter was really doing nothing radically different economically from what his immediate predecessors had done. The ideas of the men advising him, men like Charles Schultze and Alfred Kahn, hardly differed from those of the men who had advised Nixon, or even Johnson, for that matter. Sure, he was running budgetary deficits even in a recovery period when according to now accepted theory he should have run surpluses, but so had they. The difference was that this time what resulted was not a return to prosperity but what Theodore White, in his book *America in Search of Itself* (in which he chronicles modern America from Eisenhower to Reagan) terms "The Great Inflation." It produced "a contagion of fear" in the United States where "faith in one's own planning was dissolving—all across the nation. The bedrock was heaving."

That fact helped defeat Jimmy Carter and elect Ronald Reagan. Reagan promised to restore the bedrock, and the majority of Americans who voted believed him. Keynesian policies, he said, no longer worked. All they produced was 14 percent rates of inflation and 20 percent rates of interest. He was going to go back to square one, to the economics that he had been taught in a small college in the Midwest in the 1920's . . . to the *real* economics of the classicists, to free enterprise. Whether he knew it or not, he was going *all* the way back to Say's law, to Smith's invisible hand, to Marshall's equilibrium. He was going to balance the budget and rein in the supply of money and thus slay the dragon of inflation; he was going to cut taxes and deregulate the economy and thus slay the dragon of unemployment; and after he had done this, the economy would take care of itself, just as the classical economists promised it would.

But what Reagan found out was that while he could do one, he could not do the other. He, or more properly the Federal Reserve, under its chairman, Paul Volcker, did indeed rein in the money supply and produced a miracle: the runaway inflation that had Theodore White as well as the doom-and-gloom guys and the readers of their newsletters scared to death suddenly evaporated. Inflation plummeted from a high of 15 percent during Carter's mid-term down to a month-to-month rate of zero in the first quarter of 1983, and a basic underlying rate of 3 percent yearly. As inflation fell, so did the prime rate of interest, from a killing high of 21.5 percent and rising, to 11 percent and falling. Reagan had been in office for just two years, and the bedrock had been restored.

The stock market reacted with the biggest rally of the century; so did the bond market. The reasoning was that once high interest rates were eliminated, the savings that tax cuts were producing would soon be tapped by commerce and industry for investment, and that investment would produce recovery and employment and prosperity for all once again. The higher incomes that would be generated would result in higher tax receipts and eventually we would return to a balanced budget. All one had to do was stay the course, and by 1984, or at the very latest 1988, the clock would be turned back to 1954—the years of Eisenhower with 3 percent inflation, 4 percent growth and 5 percent "structural" unemployment.

Sure, recessions would recur now and again, but they would be short and "cleansing." The "normalcy" of the 1950's was once again just around the corner.

Or was it? Today Mr. Reagan and we find ourselves in a corner from which there seems to be no way out, for we are faced with an impossible choice. The inevitable cost of cutting inflation today is very high unemployment, currently still around 8 percent of the work force. Is the inevitable cost of cutting unemployment tomorrow going to be a return to high rates of inflation the day after?

That there is a tradeoff between inflation and unemployment had been sensed for a long time, but the relationship was most vividly pinned down statistically by an Australian engineer turned economist, A. W. Phillips. Phillips started not with the overall rate of inflation but rather with wages, and determined that the rate of increase in wages is inversely related to the level of unemployment in a consistent statistical manner, as shown on the lower curve in Figure 3. In plain English, if, for example, wages were rising at a rate of 7 percent in a given year, unemployment would be 6 percent. If, however, the rate of wage increases was raised to, say, 10 percent, then unemployment would fall to 5 percent. The idea, of course, gained credence that if unemployment ever rose to unacceptable levels, all we had to do was inflate ourselves out of it. As long as a little inflation evoked a lot of employment, why not a lot of inflation most of the time?

The problem is that during the past ten years there has been a dramatic upward shift in the Phillips curve as well as a change in its shape, represented by the upper curve in Figure 3. In 1979 under Carter, the 12.5 percent inflation did not bring unemployment down to 3 or 4 percent as it should have according to Phillips. Instead the jobless rate remained stuck at 7.5 percent. When Paul Volcker and the Fed attacked inflation with a single-minded vengeance, the result was not just more unemployment, but by far the most unemployment since 1940, a situation that seemed on the edge of slipping out of control. So now, it would seem, the old reliable Phillips curve has been replaced by a new and distinctly ominous one.

What can one conclude from this? My conclusion is that there has been a deep-seated *structural* change in how our economy operates. In the Carter years we learned that we could no longer "cure" unemployment by inflating the economy. But equally important, in fact maybe more important for the 1980's, we have learned under Reagan that if we try to "cure" inflation by deflating the economy through brutally tight monetary policy, the economy does not just slow down temporarily, but almost

FIGURE 3
The Phillips Curve

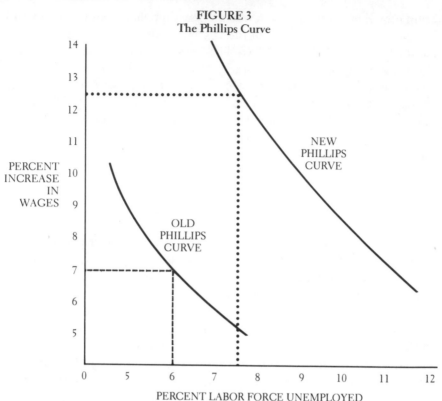

PERCENT LABOR FORCE UNEMPLOYED

collapses. We are finding out that we can't live with inflation, but we are also finding out that a lot of us—ten or twelve million of us—may be unable to live without it!

We are discovering that any change in the direction of government policy produces highly exaggerated responses; e.g., the shift from inflationary to deflationary monetary policy between 1979–80 and 1981–82 produced not just another recession, but the deepest and longest recession since the 1930's. What is particularly disturbing about this most recent "response" is that it was hardly the result of an all-out war on inflation. To be sure, during 1981–82 monetary policy was extraordinarily tight, resulting in killer interest rates which eventually caused the economy to stall and rates of inflation to tumble. But while all this was going on at the Fed, the White House and the Treasury were going in the opposite direction. They were following a highly *expansionary* fiscal policy, spending billions on defense and more billions on entitlement programs, while cutting tax rates sharply. The result was annual deficits headed, irrevocably, toward $200 billion and higher.

What, one wonders, would have happened if *both monetary and fiscal* policy had been working in tandem? What if Reagan had fulfilled his preelection promise and actually balanced the budget in 1982 by reducing the money supply and, at the same time, raising taxes and cutting the defense and entitlement budgets? My guess is that we would have ended up in a Depression, with a capital D.

Fortunately, Reagan didn't. While the people at the Fed were playing their Scrooge-like monetarist roles, Reagan's conservative Republicans at the White House were playing the unfamiliar role of super-Keynesians. Thus at one and the same time he had both the monetary brake pedal and the fiscal accelerator pressed to the floor. The result: in 1983 tight money policy had brought inflation to the lowest level in memory, loose fiscal policy produced an economic recovery that was well under way and unemployment, while still very high, was steadily declining from its earlier peaks.

So are we out of the woods for the rest of this decade?

And if we're not, what happens next?

The biggest worry, as anyone on Wall Street will tell you, is the fear of renewed inflation, especially double-digit inflation, which would result in even higher interest rates than at present. So let's first consider the future of inflation and interest rates, the deadly combination which almost took us over the brink at the beginning of the decade, and which, if they run wild again, might kill both the stock and bond markets perhaps once and for all!

Am I being paranoid even to suggest such a possibility? Is 12 percent inflation possible again in this decade? After all, the experts tell us that the one thing that Reagan did do, and do very thoroughly, was slay *that* dragon. Well, read what Milton Friedman, one of the grandfathers of Reaganomics, and the father of the monetarist school—and as well qualified as anyone to predict the future path of inflation and interest rates —said in *Barron's* in late 1982:

BARRON'S: What will rates do now?
FRIEDMAN: My own estimate, based upon monetary growth over the past two years, is that inflation will remain in the range 6%–9%, perhaps, for the next several years . . . On the other hand, there is a considerable possibility that we will reverse course, either under Chairman Volcker or his successor, and we will once again be on the upturn of an inflationary

cycle. In that case, the expectation is that the inflation rate will be somewhere between 20% and 30% five to seven years from now. If you average
that roughly, you get an inflation expectation somewhere around 10%–
13%. And that's entirely consistent with where long-term interest rates
have been.

But what about unemployment? Would renewed inflation at least put
people back to work? The Bank for International Settlements, the central
bank of the world's key central banks, gave its opinion in its 1982 annual
report. Should the Fed reflate, should it "reverse course," to use Friedman's terminology, "the belief is now widely held that, under present
conditions . . . recourse to policies of demand reflation would . . . increase
both inflation *and* unemployment" (my emphasis). The BIS, whose
economists rank among the most respected in the world, concludes: "In
the longer run lower inflation is seen as a *precondition* for lower unemployment."

But why should low inflation mean lower unemployment and high
inflation mean higher unemployment? Because, unlike their counterparts
in Brazil, where 25 to 50 percent rates of inflation have been common
for decades, our businesses, our industries, our banks, our savings and
loans, appear simply unable to cope with the dual phenomena of high
rates of inflation and high interest. For banks accustomed to fixed mortgage rates, for instance, which lend for thirty years at 10 percent and then
a few years later have to maintain their liquidity by borrowing for thirty
days at 20 percent, as the savings and loans had to do a few years ago and
will have to do again a few years hence if Friedman is right, they go broke!
If savings and loans go broke, their mortgage lending stops and the
housing industry collapses. If it collapses, then the timber industry does
likewise. The process then goes on and on as unemployment rises with
every ripple.

We simply cannot afford that again in this decade. The dilemma,
therefore, is that we seem to have arrived at a point in the history of
economic development at which both high unemployment and recurring
high rates of inflation may be endemic to the system. When a government
tries to correct one of these evils, it simply exacerbates the other. As we
have seen, when Reagan successfully reversed the inflationary trend at
least temporarily through the application of a severe monetary policy and
extraordinarily high interest rates, the result was a jump of 3 percentage
points in the rate of unemployment. When his predecessor, Carter, con-
doned very loose fiscal and monetary policies, hoping for full employment,

7.5 percent of the American labor force remained out of work while the rate of inflation doubled.

If we look at the evidence over an even longer period in the United States, spanning four presidencies and not just the last two, we are led to two rather ominous conclusions.

First, that the cyclical movements in the American economy are suddenly taking the form of increasingly wild oscillations. Look at unemployment: between 1959 and 1971 unemployment never went above 6.9 percent or below 3.4 percent, a spread of 3.5 percent. But after that, the swings really started in earnest: the 3.4 percent unemployment of 1971 soared to 8.9 percent in 1974; it fell way back down to 4.8 percent in 1975 but then swung wildly up to almost 11 percent in 1982. The spread between peaks and troughs had *doubled!*

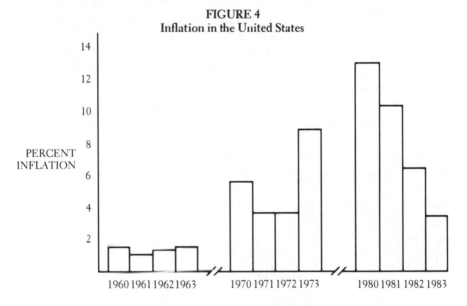

FIGURE 4
Inflation in the United States

Now look at inflation. Figure 4 shows the rates of inflation for the first four years of the 1960's, the 1970's and the 1980's—years which for the sixties and seventies seem typical of the entire decade. Between 1960 and 1963 the rate of inflation varied between a low of 0.9 percent in 1961 and a high of 1.5 percent in 1963. Inflation averaged only 2.2 percent for the entire decade. In the first four years of the 1970's the range had begun to widen, from 3.5 percent in 1971 to almost 9 percent in 1973, and the average for the decade was up to 7.5 percent. But look at what has happened in this decade: the inflation rate went from a high of almost

14 percent in 1980 to a fifteen-year low of 3 percent in 1983, and the average was up to 8.5 percent. Milton Friedman has suggested that the next upswing could take us to 20 percent or even 30 percent if we abandon the severe monetary restraint that he advocates. Just a cursory look at Figure 4 shows that the spread between the high and the low has *tripled* in comparison to earlier "normal" times. Yet Friedman suggested that the swings during the remainder of the 1980's are going to be even more pronounced—from that 3 percent rate in 1983 to 25 percent in 1988!

Second, overlaid on these increasingly wild oscillations is a secular trend (one that "overrides" the shorter-term ups and downs) which is seeing the peak levels of both inflation and unemployment mounting higher and higher in each cycle. Inflation rose from a 1960's peak of 6 percent to a 1970's peak of over 13 percent. If Friedman is right—and let me stress right here that I by no means think that he necessarily is—the 1980's peak will be in the 20 percent to 30 percent range. Likewise, unemployment relentlessly advanced from low to high single-digit figures and then at the beginning of the 1980's, like inflation, moved into double digits; but, unlike inflation, unemployment stayed there for years before starting to fall, and then only very reluctantly.

If these were two isolated phenomena, maybe we could regard the American experience during the past ten years as an aberration and forget about it.

But when we look at other capitalistic countries, the inescapable thought arises that perhaps we are facing a crisis of the system itself.

Chapter 4

o◯oo◯oo◯o

A Spreading
Economic Malaise

THE CURRENT ECONOMIC MALAISE, from which we may or may not be recovering, did not start with the United States, nor will it stop here. The timing of its onset, and its current severity, are related to levels of maturity of various national economies. To keep it simple, let's just look at three other countries: Britain, whose economy is more mature than ours; Canada, whose economic structure is very similar to that of the United States; and West Germany, which is less mature than we are, since it had to start all over again in 1945.

Now let's take a quick look at, first, whether during the past ten years the economic systems of those countries have shown signs of increasingly pronounced oscillations with respect to inflation or unemployment, and, second, whether the secular trends in those nations are also deteriorating.

First let's look at the increasingly violent inflationary oscillations. The case that best makes the point is, logically, the United Kingdom, the most mature of the Western nations. In the past ten years the inflationary ups and downs have been nothing less than wild, as Figure 5 demonstrates. Figure 6 shows that even in Canada things have not exactly been on a steady course.

Meanwhile the German experience, as one might expect, has hardly been stable but is the nearest thing to it (Figure 7).

But the experiences of other industrial countries have been much closer to those of the British, Americans and Canadians than to that of the Germans. For instance, Japan's inflation rate has varied between a high of 22 percent and a low of 3.5 percent during the past ten years; Switzer-

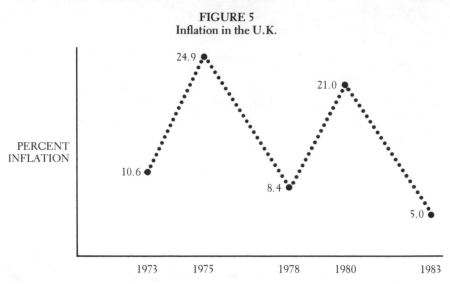

FIGURE 5
Inflation in the U.K.

land's between 11.9 percent and 0.7 percent; Finland's between 18.1 percent and 6.5 percent.

Such increasing price instability might be merely worrisome but hardly critical if it were not accompanied by a seemingly relentless deterioration in the ability of the Western economies to employ their labor forces. Look at the trend lines in Figure 8. Between 1974 and 1979, unemployment

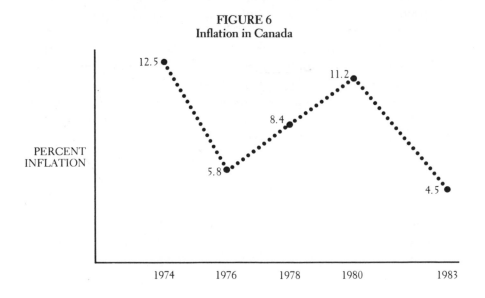

FIGURE 6
Inflation in Canada

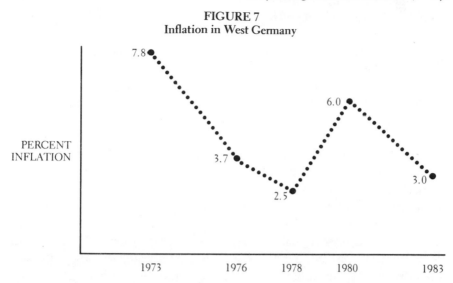

FIGURE 7
Inflation in West Germany

rates slowly but steadily increased (except for a brief respite in the United States in the 1977–79 period); then in country after country they virtually exploded on the up-side. What caused this explosion? One reason, I think, is that all these countries had been following Keynesian policies from World War II until the end of the 1970's. The Keynesian approach to

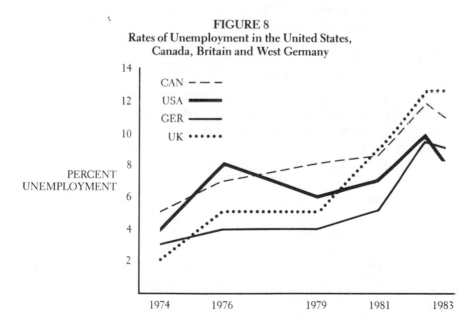

FIGURE 8
Rates of Unemployment in the United States,
Canada, Britain and West Germany

minimizing unemployment by stimulating demand through governmental intervention, a policy which had worked so well in the 1950's and 1960's, had begun to produce poorer and poorer results in the 1970's, especially where full employment was concerned.

Why? Because increasingly, government spending, financed more and more through borrowings, has been directed at so-called transfer payments—payments in small amounts to millions of individuals for everything from health care to food stamps. Such payments do little or nothing to promote investment and economic growth. They merely ensure temporary economic survival on borrowed money. Deficits promote economic growth when they result in increased demand for cars and steel and computers, as well as in savings and thus in an expansion of the "machine" that creates greater and greater wealth. Put another way, deficits are effective when they contribute to investment, as they did during World War II, thus establishing the base for postwar growth; they are not effective when they merely stimulate consumption. There is also the problem of "leakage"—demand stimulus which entices Americans to buy cars but increasingly benefits Japanese and not Americans. The purchase of Toyotas stimulates employment—in Japan—but does nothing for the ex-workers in the automotive industry in Detroit.

Most important, during the past two decades politicians have abandoned one of Lord Keynes's basic concepts. Keynes said that fiscal policy should always be *counter* cyclical, that during a recession governments should run deficits in order to create demand, but that during recoveries governments should run *surpluses* so as to dampen the inflation that is inevitably rekindled when a boom starts to get out of hand, as too much money again starts chasing too few goods. Despite this perfectly sensible advice, in twenty-three of the last twenty-four years, through every *recovery* but one, the United States has run deficits, thus *magnifying* rather than *dampening* inflationary tendencies. By the early 1980's, in fact, *all* nations had large budget deficits, so large that there was hardly room left for *further* fiscal stimulus by making them *yet* larger. On the other hand, to reduce these deficits substantially would be equally unwise, since that would jeopardize the recovery. So the neo-Keynesians had painted themselves into a corner. Many of their once fervent supporters now feel that the cumulative effect of their policies would only result in further stagflation and rising levels of unemployment.

For it has been increasingly perceived that the wild oscillations in the rate of inflation—and the enormous instability of interest rates which resulted, sending disrupting signals through the system—were a greater danger to economic well-being than unemployment. So one after the other, each of these countries sought stability by turning sharply to the right, toward supply-side theories and toward monetarism, toward higher interest rates and toward reduced social spending. As we have already noted, first came Thatcher in England, then Reagan in the United States and finally the Christian Democrat Helmut Kohl in Germany, who took over from Helmut Schmidt's Social Democrats. In each country, once the government abandoned Keynesian economics and began to apply the monetary and/or fiscal brakes, the economy "overreacted" and massive unemployment was the result.

Why? I would say it's because in one country after another the system has lost its resilience; during the past ten years or so there has been a steady, perhaps accelerating, deterioration in the system's ability to withstand shock. Any radical change in economic parameters now puts the economies of the West into either an inflationary crisis or a crisis of unemployment. We'll come to the reasons why in a moment.

What concerns us here is that the gyrations in the rates of inflation and the steady increase in the levels of unemployment have to a substantial degree been the product of three "shocks" in a row to which the system has been subjected during the past ten years: the oil embargo in 1973; the radical oil price increase in 1979; and the Thatcher/Reagan economic policy U-turns in 1980–81. The first two shocks caused violent price reactions; the third shock, which was imposed from within, produced a vast leap in unemployment. George Stigler, the conservative economist who won the 1982 Nobel Prize in economics, summed up the net result of where this all had landed us by the end of 1982: "depression" is the word he used.

The question that now faces us is this: What will happen if, or when, we are subjected to a fourth or a fifth shock later in the current decade?

But to answer that question, we must ask another one first: If we have lost our resilience, what did it consist of in the first place?

Chapter 5

o☾ooʘooʘo

Paradise Lost

THE RESILIENCE OF OUR ECONOMIC SYSTEM—its ability to grow under the stress of constantly changing conditions—is of such fundamental importance to our economic future that it can hardly be stressed enough. Sustained economic growth, while it lasted, was the Great Shock Absorber. Economic growth allowed us to shrug off such shocks as the onset of the Cold War in 1947–48; the onset of the Korean War in 1950–51; the onset of the Vietnam War in 1965–66; and the Penn Central collapse and the closing of the gold window in 1971. Not only could our society *accommodate* these "shocks"; between 1947 and 1971 the output of the capitalistic world *grew* more than at any other time in human history, shocks and all.

But look what happened to economic growth in the four countries we've been examining (the United States, the United Kingdom, Canada, West Germany) after the first oil shock hit in the last quarter of 1973 (Figure 9). This shock stopped economic growth instantaneously! Worse, in every case it took each country *three years* just to get back to where it had been in October 1973 when it got hit with the embargo.

Figure 10 shows what happened after the second oil shock in 1979. Same thing! Stagnation in output resulted, and lasted for *another* three years.

Now look what happened when the monetary shock was imposed in the United States, sending interest rates soaring around the globe (Figure 11). The result of this monetary shock was even more devastating than the two prior oil shocks.

If it takes years for the advanced economies to resume growth after

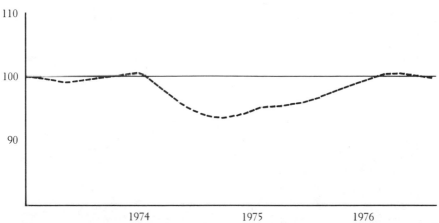

FIGURE 9
Industrial Output in Four Countries
Last quarter of 1973 (oil embargo) = 100

being shocked by oil price increases or extreme monetary restraint, can it be that perhaps the *preconditions* for growth are either lost or seriously impaired? In other words, is it possible that the shocks are not the problem but that it's the health of the economy that's to blame? Could it be that, like a lot of us who have grown older, these mature economies can no longer shake off a cold as easily as they used to, much less the flu, much less still pneumonia?

What were the preconditions for growth, which allowed for a doubling,

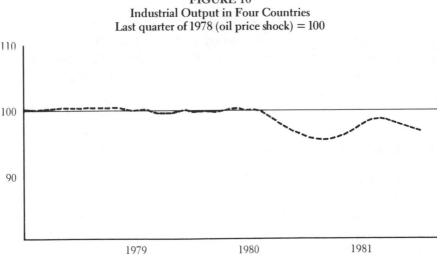

FIGURE 10
Industrial Output in Four Countries
Last quarter of 1978 (oil price shock) = 100

FIGURE 11
Industrial Output in Four Countries
End of 1980 (U.S. hits the monetary brakes) = 100

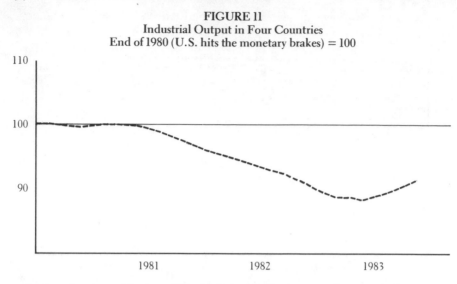

at least, of our wealth since World War II? Or put another way, what were the economic props whose removal could put the system into a state of shock, and then of stagnation?

They were:

· low energy costs
· sustained low rates of inflation
· sustained low rates of interest
· rapidly expanding world trade
· a viable, integrated, global banking system

If such preconditions have already disappeared (as in the case of cheap energy) or if they are seriously endangered (as in the case of sustainable low rates of both inflation and interest) or if they are now increasingly threatened (as in the case of both free trade and the viability of the international banking system), then economic growth, as a general, pre-dictable, overall condition under which we all can expect to live, has been lost.

Equally important, for the first time in our history we seem to have run out of innovations powerful enough to compensate for the loss of the so-called prerequisites cited above, new ways of creating wealth to serve as new sources of global growth.

What we are talking about here is really only a variation on the old frontier theory. The discovery of the New World brought enormous prosperity to the Old World in the seventeenth century, just as the exploitation of the western frontier enriched America in the nineteenth century. In our century, specifically since World War II, we have been fortunate to have benefited from a series of "mini" frontiers. The Marshall Plan in essence created a new frontier out of the advanced industrial economies of the Old World. Instantaneously it galvanized the massive recovery of Western Europe. What resulted was a global increase in demand for everything from foodstuffs to iron ore to coal to Camel cigarettes, of a magnitude never before seen. The ripple effect as this prosperity returned across the Atlantic to the United States cannot be underestimated as one of the key reasons for those "good years" under Eisenhower.

The Marshall Plan "effect" had no sooner begun to ebb than it was replaced by the vastly stimulating process of European economic integration which followed the signing of the Treaty of Rome in 1957, the treaty that provided the framework for the Common Market. The emergence of a market of 250 million consumers that could be served from a central manufacturing source spurred investment in new plant and equipment, funded to a substantial degree by American-based multinational corporations, on a scale unprecedented in modern times. As a result, the real rate of economic growth doubled in most European countries and remained high for many years. The *Wirtschaftswunder* of Germany, the economic miracle of Italy, the amazingly high rates of economic growth achieved by France generated yet another economic ripple effect that was as beneficial to the copper mines of the Congo and Chile, the cocoa producers of Ghana or the bauxite mines of Quebec as it was to Volkswagen, Olivetti and Philips of the "host" European continent itself, from which this new growth impulse came. For the United States it meant that by the late 1960's many of its largest corporations were earning more in Europe than they were back home . . . a circumstance unprecedented in the history of a nation that considered itself a self-sufficient "island" economy.

The principal investment consequence of this extended period of post-war growth was that it produced an equally extended bull market on Wall Street. Wall Street had experienced rising prices from 1941 through 1945, but in 1946 the wartime bull market ended. Investors were afraid that wartime boom might very well be followed by peacetime bust—as had happened so often in financial history. As a result, after the Dow Jones Industrial Average hit the 200 mark in early 1946, it backed off and stayed below that level for the next three years. Then, however, spurred by the economic growth promoted by the Marshall Plan and further encouraged by the outbreak of the Korean War, the market moved through that 200 level in 1950 and then through 300 in 1954. As the economic boom began to embrace all of Western Europe in the pull of the creation of the Common Market, there seemed to be no end in sight for prosperity in the Atlantic Community. The economic ebullience of that era was reflected in the Dow rising ever higher, finally peaking at 1,000 in the early days of 1966. But even when economic growth around the Atlantic began to cool off, though the market also cooled off, it by no means collapsed.

For in this same period the whole world benefited from a third—though much more controversial—impetus to growth: the emergence of Japan as a major global economic power, one that devoured everything from soybeans to timber to petroleum as its output skyrocketed. All that everybody had hoped China might be some day to the Western economies—a huge customer and a vast supplier—and never has been, was now being accomplished by a small chain of islands with only 100 million people.

But by the early 1980's the stimulative effects of all three phenomena have subsided. In fact, it is increasingly perceived by many that the further rise of Japan and its progressive takeover of ever larger market shares, with one product after the other, in one continent after the other, is now counterproductive to the other developed countries, so that a new wave of protectionistic sentiment has arisen which may seriously undermine one of the crucial preconditions to growth—global free trade.

Finally, we all benefited enormously from the effects of the so-called Second Industrial Revolution—the increasing introduction of automation to industrial processes, which allowed output to rise in tandem with the enormous increase of demand evoked first by the Marshall Plan, then by the economic integration of Europe and then by the emergence of the new Japan. Had Keynes and Say lived through the 1950's and 1960's, each might have been convinced that he was right: governmentally engineered economic innovations evoked enormous growth in demand; that demand, in turn, evoked a technological revolution which made possible an enormous expansion of output providing both full employment and stable prices, thus vindicating both Keynes and what was to be called supply-side economics.

But by the 1980's we are left with one great hope—the technological revolution in electronics and genetic engineering, and the productivity benefits and new wealth that these new technologies promise to bring. I believe that this hope is justified—and I will say more on this subject later. But for now, I fear that the "salvation" promised by high technology may only come slowly, and that it might be a matter of decades, not years, before Silicon Valley will generate growth sufficient to fill the enormous gap being left by the deindustrialization of the West, especially where employment is concerned. Such considerations have led the Western Europeans to greet this new frontier with mixed emotions. After all, it is the application of robotics in Japan that has cost the jobs of hundreds of thousands of European workers in the electronics, shipbuilding and automotive industries. Why, the Europeans are asking, increase output through higher productivity when there is no longer sufficient demand— because there is no longer sufficient employment—to absorb it? So it is that with ever-increasing caution these labor-saving innovations are being introduced there. And thus there is legitimate doubt as to whether even the growth-enhancing effects of technological innovation will spread through the capitalistic system in this decade, or even in this century, to a degree sufficient to restore our former resilience.

Thus both the sources of and the preconditions for sustained economic growth in the capitalistic world seem to be lacking, at least for now. With the healing power for growth absent, the vulnerability of the system to shocks is high, and probably increasing.

What would be the consequences of our being hit by yet another shock, or series of shocks? And are there likely to be such new shocks in the foreseeable future?

Chapter 6

o〇oo〇oo〇o

The
Bank Crisis

A S I HAVE INDICATED, a key precondition for economic growth is the solvency of the financial institutions that are the foundation upon which our capitalistic system rests. Put more bleakly, if the banking system were to collapse, the consequences would be devastating.

Let's go directly to the point: Is it possible that during this decade, or during our lifetime, we could actually experience a major, worldwide banking collapse, a shock that would relegate to the minor leagues the three previous "shocks" that have stunned our system into stagnation during the past dozen years? Or is the thought of such a catastrophe only worthy of the lunatic fringe?

The voice of the financial establishment, the *Wall Street Journal*, in a rare moment of humor suggested that the world's banks have come to the edge of a great abyss . . . and are about to take a great leap forward. In fact, it could be argued that the current condition of the banks is an almost inevitable consequence of the collapse of that growth-nurturing economic framework—made up, as we have seen, of low energy costs, steady rates of interest, expanding world trade and so on.

Today the word that haunts every banker on every continent is *default*!

The size of potential defaults facing the men running Chase Manhattan of New York or Continental Illinois of Chicago or the Royal Bank of Canada in Toronto or the Dresdner Bank in Frankfurt are of staggering proportions. To put the current situation into perspective, if just one more major country, Brazil, a borderline case, were to join three other countries already in de facto default, namely Mexico, Argentina and Poland, the

Western financial system would be holding the bag for this foursome to the extent of $231 billion—$231,000,000,000. If you then add in what the Third World and Eastern Europe owe to us, both of which regions are financial basket cases almost in their entirety, you end up with a grand total of $735 billion owed to Western and Japanese banks by countries unlikely to pay even the interest on what they owe.

American banks are probably on the line for a third of this. And it is the ten largest banks in the United States, the so-called money center banks, which are owed the lion's share of that. To show how exposed they are: the total combined capital, or shareholders' equity, of these ten banks is around $22.6 billion. When a bank loses its capital, it must by law close its doors. One country alone, Mexico, owes these ten banks $12.9 billion, or almost exactly 57 percent of that buffer which stands between them and bankruptcy. Mexico is broke. If, in addition to Mexico, you add the exposure that these same banks have in two other countries, Brazil and Venezuela, you see that it is not unusual for a large American bank to have over 125 percent of its equity at risk in just three financially shaky Latin American nations (see Table 1). This is the reason why a lot of bankers today may wish they had become novelists, as I did.

So how did the world's banks get into this mess? As with so many of

TABLE 1

The Exposure of the Ten Largest American Banks in Mexico, Brazil and Venezuela at the End of 1982*

	MEXICAN EXPOSURE (as Percent of Capital)	COMBINED EXPOSURE IN MEXICO, BRAZIL AND VENEZUELA (as Percent of Capital)
Citibank	54.6	146.3
Bank of America	52.1	141.7
Chase Manhattan	40.0	120.9
Morgan Guaranty	34.8	106.6
Manufacturers Hanover	66.7	186.8
Continental Illinois	32.4	76.9
Chemical	60.0	140.0
First Interstate	63.0	125.4
Security Pacific	31.2	64.8
Bankers Trust	46.2	117.5

These # seemed to be reduced by 10% (1986).

*Information is drawn from William R. Cline, *International Debt and the Stability of the World Economy*, Institute for International Economics, Policy Analysis in International Economics, No. 4, September 1983, p. 34, Table 6.

→ reduce down a lot but they have high tech debt!
→ ↑ capital ratio on all these banks but not classify the loans like they do on normal loans. 1—5
good loan → worst loan.

the world's woes, it all began in 1973 with oil. When the price went from $2 to $10 a barrel, a lot of poor countries that happened to have oil got rich overnight—like Saudi Arabia and Kuwait and Venezuela and Nigeria, i.e., the so-called lesser-developed countries or LDCs—while a lot of other nations without oil got poor or poorer—like Zaire, or Argentina, or Pakistan. The former group was piling up oil income much faster than it could spend it, while the latter countries were suddenly paying energy import bills five times the size they had been used to, draining even further their limited foreign-exchange resources.

The obvious solution would have been for the *rich* LDCs with oil to lend some of their surplus dollars to the *poor* LDCs. But that would have been too logical. Plus the fact that the Arabs are not dumb. Why risk lending money to basket cases?

Enter creative financing, masterminded by the hotshots from Chase and Citibank and Manufacturers Hanover. Lend the money to us, they told the fellows in Riyadh, and *we* will lend it to the basket cases.

Sovereign loans are what they called them. And their reasoning was this: people go broke; companies go broke; even banks, God help us, sometimes go broke—but countries *never* do. Right? How safe can you get? And who else can borrow billions at one crack and thus save you the enormous amount of paperwork that comes when all you are lending is millions? Only countries, that's who. So let's borrow from the Saudis and lend to the basket cases and make a few points in between—make a few million in profit—on the transaction.

So the immense supply of surplus petrodollars created its own demand in the form of sovereign loans. Oil money poured into the banks from OPEC countries and the men in their pinstriped suits got onto Pan Am and headed for darkest Africa, remotest Latin America, searching for sovereign nations who would take some of those billions off their hands —at a few percentage points over the rate they were paying the Arabs, plus enormous front-end fees. The pinstripes found their customers quickly enough. Peru took a couple of billion. Brazil took a couple of tens of billions. Zaire, Argentina, Costa Rica, Pakistan—the list seemed endless. Then the bankers of Germany, fearing that their greedy American competitors were about to wrap up the whole world, discovered Eastern Europe. Hell, if Brazil was good for $40 billion, Poland must be good for at least $20 billion. And if Poland was good for twenty, then Rumania and Hungary must be good for ten.

So it went between 1973 and 1977. By the end of that period, Western bank loans to LDCs and Eastern Europe had gone from almost scratch to over $250 billion. Then came the second oil "shock." The price of crude, which had seemingly stabilized in the $10 range, suddenly zoomed to $20 a barrel, then $30, then $40. The OPEC surpluses quadrupled. And there was not an energy expert on earth who was not firmly, indisputably, irrevocably forecasting that $60 and then $80 and then $100 a barrel were inevitable, probably by as early as the mid-1980's. Which meant that there would be money galore gushing out of the Arabian peninsula into the hands of the world's bankers ad infinitum. So they scrambled around the world ever faster, lining up takers willing to pledge their countries, maybe now for the tenth time, as collateral for yet another sovereign loan. Result: between 1977 and 1980 the banks *doubled* their borrowings from the Arabs and also *doubled* their lendings to the LDCs and Communist Europe—bringing the grand total to well over one half trillion dollars.

Then came a new wrinkle. Heretofore the oil-producing LDCs had been the *suppliers* of funds to the banks, and the non-oil-producing LDCs had been the borrowers of the same funds from the same banks. Beginning in 1979 that changed. Nigeria, Mexico, Venezuela—oil-rich nations if there ever were such—suddenly decided that if the price of oil was inevitably headed toward $100 a barrel, then they might as well lie back and enjoy it. Emulate the Yankees' formula for success: buy now, pay later.

So they embarked upon massive development programs financed fifty-fifty cash/debt—one half still coming from their current oil income; the other half now financed by the external borrowing of dollars from the banks of the developed world. Mexico borrowed $91 billion; Venezuela borrowed $36 billion; Indonesia got $22 billion; Nigeria $10 billion.

As a result Mexico became the fastest-growing nation on earth. Venezuela was second. Everybody was happy, especially the bankers. What better borrowers could be found than sovereign states with the highest economic growth rates on earth and hundreds of billions of dollars worth of oil in the ground?

And then came the oil glut.

The oil price, instead of soaring from $40 a barrel to $60 a barrel as everybody said it would, went back down to $35, then $32, then $29. The projected oil income of the oil-producing LDCs collapsed along with the price. The resulting problem was compounded by the fact that these countries had borrowed short-term even though the development projects they were financing were, by definition, of a long-term nature. Thus in 1982 alone Mexico was committed to repay the banks of the developed world $29.2 billion in the form of either interest or short-term debt which had already come due. They paid neither. For Mexico had lost all its gold and dollar reserves because its more "prudent" millionaires had already sent their capital out of the country, and its oil income in 1982 was only $14 billion. So the Mexican government had no choice but to join the list of nations that had already gone into default in that critical year of 1982 when the global financial house started to fall apart.

In order of the magnitude of their de facto default, the countries that are effectively bankrupt now include: Mexico, Argentina, Poland, Rumania, Peru, Vietnam, Costa Rica, the Sudan, Zaire, Bolivia, Pakistan, Togo, Senegal, Honduras, Madagascar, Guyana, Malawi, Sierra Leone, Uganda, Liberia and the Central African Republic.

TABLE 2
The World's Biggest Debtors
In Billions of Dollars

COUNTRY	TOTAL DEBT	LOANS FROM PRIVATE BANKS
Brazil	91.0	68.5
Mexico	81.0	68.0
Argentina	36.6	27.5
Venezuela	35.5	29.0
South Korea	35.0	21.4
Poland	26.0	24.0 ·
Indonesia	21.9	9.6
Egypt	19.0	5.5
Chile	18.2	12.0
Philippines	18.0	11.6
Colombia	10.5	6.4
Thailand	10.2	6.0 ·
Nigeria	10.0	8.0

[handwritten annotation: from multinational banks.]

To provide a measure of how rapidly this crisis has developed: As late as 1978 the only countries on earth that were in default were Peru and Turkey, and the grand amount involved was a paltry $2.3 billion.

The reasons that each of these countries has had to renege on its financial commitments were all somewhat different: Argentina because of a war, Poland because of its vast misguided overinvestment in heavy industry, Honduras because the coffee price went sour, Zaire because nobody in the government there has a clue as to how to run a country. But the result was the same in all cases: insufficient dollar income and/or reserves to service their dollar debts.

Are they ever going to be able to repay? If not, who or what is going to bail them out? If there is no bailout, which banks in which countries are likely to go belly up?

Let's answer the last question first. The American banks that have lent the mostest to the weakest are the biggest ones we have: Citibank, Chase Manhattan, Continental Illinois, Bank of America, Morgan Guaranty, Manufacturers Hanover, Chemical Bank, First Interstate, Security Pacific, Bankers Trust. Why? First, simply because they are the ten biggest banks in the United States. And because of their size they were automatically on the list of the fifty largest banks in the world, those banks which the Arabs considered eligible to receive almost unlimited amounts of petrodollar deposits. The vast supply of money thus put at their disposal created its own pressure to find demand for equal amounts. Thus the proliferation of sovereign loans on such an immense scale by such few banks. The other reason: greed. Every one of these banks today makes half of its profits abroad, give or take a few percentage points. Ten years ago not one did.

Now to the bailout issue. What if things suddenly get worse? For instance, what if everybody in the developing world plus most of Eastern Europe decides to get on the default bandwagon simultaneously, openly, and defiantly; or on a much less flamboyant level, what if some bank examiner, somewhere, overcome by conscience, decides to declare these bad loans as—bad loans—thus forcing one of the big banks in New York or London or Frankfurt to the wall? Will Uncle Sam simply stand aside and let Citibank or Chase or Continental Illinois go broke? Will the Bank of England deliberately allow a Barclays or a National Westminster or a Lloyds to go belly up? Will the Bundesbank let the Dresdner Bank and the Bank für Gemeinwirtschaft go down the drain? Because all of these big international banks are also in the global top fifty, all have been doing the same things as Chase or Citibank, and thus they are all exposed.

The answer is: Of course not. And the reason can be found in one shared memory: that of the Creditanstalt. The Creditanstalt was the huge Austrian bank that was allowed to go broke in 1931, which toppled financial institutions around the world and in the end resulted in the closing of ten thousand banks in the U.S. alone, banks that would never again reopen their doors. This, not the famous New York stock market crash of '29, was the single financial happening that turned a *recession*, which began in the fall of 1929, into the Great *Depression*, which lasted until 1940. No government is going to allow that to happen again. In fact, no *American* government is going to allow any *other* government ever to let it happen again.

→ This led to recession in the 30's that further led to depression.

How?

Well, first of all, by making sure that the world's commercial banks continue to throw good money after bad in order to prevent the de facto defaults on sovereign loans from turning into de jure defaults. If Brazil can't pay interest on its old loans, the banks simply process a new loan or stretch out the old ones so that it can. Ditto when the principal comes due.

How did our government coerce our commercial banks into doing this? Easy: through blackmail. The monetary authorities of the United States simply called a meeting of the key American commercial bankers and told —not asked—them to increase their net lending to LDCs on the "critical" list by 7 percent per annum. In other words, since Mexico owed Chase $1.5 billion, Chase now had to lend Mexico an additional $105 million in 1983 as a first installment. And if Chase did not go along with this "madness"? Then the United States government would take a new look at those old loans the bank had made to Mexico, loans which they were keeping alive and well on their books at 100 percent of value with the agreement of the governmental banking oversight authorities. However, it was now told them, maybe after we take a *new* look, half of these outstanding amounts will have to be written off as bad debts, eating up the banks' profits for the next three or more years. Chase and everybody else got the message and immediately proceeded to do what they were told. They do not claim, however, that they are victims of blackmail. They prefer to think of it as a process evoked for the purpose of establishing synergy between the private and public lenders of last resort.

This sort of thing worries some people. As a result, increasing numbers of investors in the United States have joined the "flight to quality" by moving their funds out of the large American banks and into Treasury bills, notes and bonds of the United States government. Abroad, this capital flight has taken the form of, paradoxically, immense purchases of U.S. dollars and a continuing move into gold, keeping its price irrationally high by historical standards in a world where rates of inflation have been universally plummeting.

The banks and bankers pretend not to be worried. Walter Wriston, chairman of Citicorp, has suggested that the debts of the LDCs and Eastern Europe should be considered more or less like the trillion-dollar national debt here in the United States, i.e., one that must be constantly "rolled over" since it will never be paid back. What Wriston did *not* point out was that while our government can print any amount of dollars it needs to service the national debt, since "we owe it to ourselves," the

[handwritten margin note: Iput continue lending to LDC's]

governments of Mexico or Argentina cannot. Unfortunately for them and for their international bankers, they owe dollars but all they can print are pesos.

So where will the dollars eventually have to come from when the rescheduling process breaks down—as it ultimately must one day? We already know the answer: the World Bank and the International Monetary Fund. The United States government and the governments of Western Europe and Japan are already in the process of increasing the capital of these international lending institutions by ten of billions of dollars. The capital of the IMF alone has gone from $66.8 billion to $98.5 billion (the funds coming directly from the pockets of the developed world's taxpayers). On top of that, these institutions themselves will now borrow additional tens of billions both from central banks of the industrialized North and in the world's capital markets (forcing high interest rates higher for the rest of us), and as the various sovereign loan default crises arise, the huge sums thus accumulated will be lent to the treasuries and central banks of the basket-case nations so that they can, in turn, pay back the money they owe Chase and Bank of America and Lloyds and the Dresdner Bank, thus maintaining their solvency and thus also precluding a rerun of the Creditanstalt collapse and its inevitable aftermath.

The United States government has proposed and the IMF is establishing a further supplemental arrangement: a special "standby" facility, a safety net with an initial funding of $19 billion which could be activated literally overnight if a real biggie, like, say, Brazil, went to the wall. Finally, the IMF has an ultimate fall-back resource in the form of the 103 million ounces of gold that it owns. But even that process has its limits. At some point the parliaments and taxpayers of the world will refuse to foot the bill any longer for the bailout of the world's private banks. The extreme reluctance of Congress to go along with the 1983 increase does not bode well for any future bailouts via the IMF. From the borrower's side, the precariousness of the situation was emphasized in October 1983, when the servicing of Argentina's $37 billion external debt was temporarily stopped by a court order issued by a thirty-nine-year-old judge sitting in an obscure provincial town 600 kilometers south of Buenos Aires. He claimed that Argentina's sovereignty was being threatened by the terms of these loans, which had just been renegotiated by the head of Argentina's central bank.

The seriousness of the situation is compounded by the fact that the ominous possibility of default is by no means restricted to sovereign loans in the process of going from bad to worse. The same banks that have their necks stuck out a mile vis-à-vis countries around the world often also have very serious problems at home. In the United States this was illustrated in the summer of 1981 by the collapse of Drysdale Securities, an obscure dealer in government securities, which suddenly went under, leaving Chase Manhattan, which had been involved in the financing of its inventory of securities, out a quarter of a billion dollars.

Then in the summer of '82 came the collapse of an equally obscure financial institution in Oklahoma City, the Penn Square Bank. Not only did large depositors in that bank lose $200 million, but it turned out that Penn Square had "sold" to such northern banks as Continental Illinois of Chicago and Seafirst Bank of Seattle, the largest bank in the Pacific Northwest, a couple of *billion* dollars of loans to oil exploration companies —loans which, for the most part, will never be repaid. Seafirst alone ended up with nearly half a billion dollars of such loans on its books. Understandably, as word of this got around, depositors started to yank their money out. As the crisis grew, top management quit, and the board of directors hurriedly hired the former head of California's Wells Fargo Bank, Richard Cooley, to help them save the bank. Within a week Cooley had gotten a consortium of the largest banks in the United States to lend Seafirst $1.5 billion to replace the $1.5 billion that nervous depositors had already withdrawn. This should have restored confidence in the institution. It didn't. So in order to keep Seafirst afloat and to calm the restless public, the only workable solution was to find a very large, *solvent* bank to take over Seafirst. The world's largest bank, Bank of America, did so in the spring of 1983 and prevented the unthinkable from happening.

Lurking in the wings is International Harvester, which had debts of $3.4 billion due at the end of 1983, of which it owed the big banks $1.4 billion in term loans. At present it is difficult to see how the company can possibly repay what it owes. Its net worth is already nearing zero, and it is still losing money. Or did you ever hear of a company called GHR? It's in the oil and gas business, is based in Good Hope, Louisiana, and because of the oil glut is also in serious financial difficulties. When its troubles surfaced in late 1982 we learned that it owed Continental Illinois $165 million; it owed Chase $125 million; it even owed a French bank, the Banque de Paris et des Pays-Bas, $245 million! How much of that they will ever get back remains to be seen.

Not that the United States situation is by any means unique. Take Canada—staid, steady Canada. Its banks are in even greater trouble because each of the top five Canadian banks has loaned over half of all its capital and reserves to just one company—Dome Petroleum (something no American bank could do, by the way, since by law no amount greater than 10 percent of a bank's capital can be lent to one borrower. In Canada there are no limits). They did so when, following the "Canadianization" policy of Prime Minister Pierre Trudeau where his country's energy industry was concerned, Dome Petroleum was encouraged to borrow billions in order to buy out foreign interests in a number of Canadian oil companies, especially Hudson's Bay Oil. It seemed like a sure thing because, after all, the oil price was going from $40 a barrel to $60 to $100. Remember? Well, wrong again. As a result of the oil glut, Dome Petroleum's income (like Mexico's) is way below what it expected and its debts (like Mexico's) are enormous, $6.3 billion. Consequently Dome (like Mexico) was forced to renege on a payment of $1.3 billion due the banks, forcing them to "restructure" and "reschedule" the debt. But this hardly solves the problem. If this default becomes total—who will bail out the Canadian banks? We already know the answer: the Canadian government, which triggered the entire mess in the first place. And it will probably do so by engineering a forced "buyout" of Dome's shareholders for ten cents on the dollar. But at what ultimate cost? Canada's development has always been financed by foreign investors. After this debacle, how many foreign investors will ever invest in Canadian banks and oil companies again? I won't.

A footnote to the Canadian situation: these same top five banks have also lent $4.7 billion to Mexico, $4.5 billion to Brazil and $1.2 billion to Argentina. About the only area where they seem to have kept their heads was in Eastern Europe: they lent just $300 million to Poland.

How will all this end?

There really is just one, and only one, "ultimate" solution: that which would be provided by a broadly based and sustained economic recovery throughout the Western world. If the three "locomotives" of global economic growth, the United States, West Germany and Japan, really got going again, they would lift the whole world up with them in the future just as they have done repeatedly in the past. Demand prices for everything from copper to cocoa to sugar to oil would recover. So would demand for International Harvester's trucks, perhaps bailing that company out if it did not come too late. But most important of all, in the pull of such a recovery the foreign-trade income of all the debtor nations would revive and they would once again have sufficient dollars to service their external debts. At least for a while.

If, however, the current economic recovery in the United States fizzles, especially if it fizzles soon, these teetering corporations and those destitute debtor nations will have no chance. The banks will have to foreclose at home. And abroad the World Bank and the IMF will someday run out of financial Band-Aids. The "temporary cash flow" problems of the Third World and Eastern Europe will then be recognized for what they really are: deep-seated *structural* problems of such magnitude that they are unsolvable in our generation.

The world would then face a default situation dwarfing that which began in 1931. If realization of this were suddenly to spread, the world's banks—all of them—could become suspect overnight. Depositors everywhere would try to get their money out at the same time. It could all happen so fast that before the governments of the world could respond by "reliquefying" the banks with "new" money, the worst would already have occurred. A riot in Mexico City could lead to revolution within days, maybe even hours. The first act of a new radical left-wing regime there would probably be to thumb its nose at the United States and its banks, not necessarily in that order. Then what? Do the bankers invade?

To be sure, there is no doubt a great temptation to view all this with a good amount of *Schadenfreude.* After all, when were moneychangers ever the most beloved among us? However, my suggestion is that you be nice to your banker. Sympathize with him. Buy him a drink now and then. Be *supportive.* <u>Because, let's face it—if *he* goes, we *all* go</u>.

Chapter 7

o◯oo◯oo◯o

The Debt Crisis

I F THE BANKERS have brought the financial world to the edge of an abyss as a result of their sovereign lending to basket cases around the world, politicians have led the rest of us into a financial swamp by creating a still worse quagmire of sovereign debt into which we all may soon sink and disappear. Where it is the word "default" that strikes fear in the hearts and minds of bankers, it is the word "deficit" that is doing the same to everybody else of sound mind who fears that unless our governments do something quickly to stem the rising tide of deficit spending, we may soon return to 13 percent inflation and 20 percent interest rates and eventually a global financial crisis which will make the current banking crisis look like fun.

For if the Mexicos and Brazils and Polands of the underdeveloped world have been living on borrowed time, propped up only by ill-advised loans from abroad, all countries of the industrialized world, from the United States to France to Canada, have been doing the same, similarly propped up by borrowing—and borrowing on a scale of such awesome proportions that if it continues it can, and must, undermine the entire system. The threat that the foreign debts of the LDCs today pose to the world's stability would then be replaced tomorrow by a global debt crisis that would embrace the entire West.

All of us are now living well beyond our means. Worse, we all are committed to continue to do so, with no end in sight. We have chosen no longer to operate government on a pay-as-you-go basis. Therefore all governments, today without a single known exception, must continue to borrow ever-increasing amounts. Mexico must, otherwise Chase Manhattan goes broke. The United States must, otherwise its defense system, and that of the West, will collapse. Germany must, otherwise its social security system will start falling apart. If that falls apart, so does the social fabric of the nation that now has 2.3 million people out of work (over 9 percent of the labor force) who are scared to death of their future—something that is not only true of Germany, where the concept of social security was born, but similarly true of millions of Belgians and Dutch and even Norwegians. Their rising unrest today haunts political leaders throughout Western Europe . . . and even Japan, whose public debt already amounts to 40 percent of GNP; just to pay the interest on that huge sum means that its government must borrow massive amounts.

Thus the imperative for the world's governments in the 1980's is: Borrow or sink.

The problem is: *Where is all the money going to come from?*

Before we come to the answer—and there is a definitive answer—let's pursue the question of how this state of affairs developed in the first place. We already know the answer where Mexico and Brazil and Costa Rica are concerned: they embarked upon overambitious development programs based on the premise that both world economic growth and the price of oil would continue onward and upward forever. Neither did, as we now know, and catastrophe looms for them and their bankers. But what about the governments of the United States and France and Italy? How did they too become dependent upon borrowing for survival?

The genesis of the problem predates the first oil embargo and, in fact, goes back to the years 1965 and 1971. If it was the Arabs and OPEC who triggered our economic crises in the 1970's by precipitating the two oil shocks, it was Presidents Johnson and Nixon who prepared the way for them. Johnson, upon assuming the presidency, decided to fight a major war in Vietnam and introduce revolutionary social programs in the United States at the same time. He also decided that both could be accomplished without raising taxes and also without the government having to engage in massive borrowings on the capital markets. Between the end of 1965 and 1970, of the $68 billion in new U.S. government debt, only $9 billion was bought by the private sector. Johnson raised the rest essentially by printing money. The procedure was for him to tell the Treasury to issue debt and convince the Federal Reserve to buy it. In technical jargon, Johnson monetized the vast majority of the new debt. As a result federal debt held by the Fed rose 50 percent, a sure-fire way to fuel inflation.

Thus, when Nixon assumed office, inflation had become a serious problem for the first time since World War II. But Nixon could have stopped it had he not put the second nail in the American financial coffin by closing the gold window on August 15, 1971, ending the convertibility of the dollar into gold. Although few people realized it at the time, that stroke of Nixon's pen ended any necessity for future monetary and price discipline in the United States, or anywhere else. This is not to fault Nixon. The crisis of the moment really allowed no other solution.

Under the old rules (those established at the Bretton Woods conference at the end of World War II), when a wave of inflation developed in any major country and its citizens started buying cheaper goods produced abroad, resulting in major outflows of that nation's currency, two courses of action lay open to its government. The government could restore international equilibrium either by slamming on the monetary brakes at home, thus halting domestic inflation and solving the problem, or by simply devaluing its currency—making foreign goods more expensive overnight and stemming the currency outflow. Both approaches would, of course, be traumatic. Hitting the monetary brakes meant high interest rates, recession and unemployment—in that sequence. Devaluation made a currency suspect for many a year thereafter, as the British found out when they dropped sterling's value from $2.80 to $2.40 in October 1967 (an event that in retrospect was the precursor of the monetary chaos which was to follow). Since sterling could now no longer be "trusted," international investors who had traditionally kept their funds in London now placed them elsewhere for fear of a second devaluation. This caused the sterling money and capital markets to shrink, and made borrowing in sterling more expensive, thus hurting the economic status of the entire nation.

The one currency that was considered inviolable was the United States dollar, for it was the benchmark for all other currencies. This inviolability of the dollar was guaranteed by the fact that it was the world's one and only currency that was directly linked to gold. That link meant that if, because of some extended period of monetary and fiscal irresponsibility in Washington, the dollar lost its purchasing power as a result of inflation inside America, then any foreign government holding dollars could freely exchange them for that ultimate store of value, gold, at the fixed price of thirty-five bucks for one ounce.

That necessity never arose. The United States was as disciplined a nation in monetary and fiscal terms as any on earth, as disciplined as

Japan, West Germany and Switzerland. The best-to-best rates of exchange never changed. The yen/dollar rate stayed at 360 for decades, the mark/dollar rate at 4. The Swiss franc/dollar rate stayed at 4.30 as if the rate had been ordained by God. When I was banking in Switzerland, as late as 1970 the Swiss central bank considered making loans in dollars exactly as safe as making them in Swiss francs. Thus no forward "cover" was required even though the deposits of Swiss banks were almost all in francs while a good percentage of their loans were in dollars.

But then in 1971, as a result of the inflation arising from Johnson's fiscal and monetary folly, the United States' trade balance went negative. For the first time since 1893 we were importing more than we were exporting. Foreigners, who are much more sensitive to changes in international trade and money flows, soon reached the conclusion that a fundamental shift had occurred; that, therefore, the dollar was no longer a sure thing as a store of value. So collectively and rapidly and led by France, they decided to trade in a substantial proportion of their inventories of now suspect dollars—they were holding around fifty billion of them at that point—for gold. Rather than see Fort Knox wiped out, Nixon suspended dollar/gold convertibility. He had no other choice.

Now it was the United States that faced the alternative of curing the problem either by dumping the American economy into deep recession via monetary policy or by devaluing the dollar. The Nixon Administration opted for devaluation. But as Ezra Solomon, who at that time was a member of Nixon's Council of Economic Advisers, points out in his truly excellent recent book, *Beyond the Turning Point*, nobody in Washington knew how to do it!

Changing the dollar/gold price wouldn't accomplish anything, since this relationship was meaningless now that no government could trade in its dollars for gold. Thus the White House finally concluded that, in fact, it could *not* be done unilaterally. The only way to *devalue* the dollar (i.e., *reduce* its exchange value) was to talk all the other countries that counted into revaluing *their* currencies (i.e., *increasing* their exchange value relative to the dollar). Put bluntly, what the Americans were looking for was the yen not at 360 but at 300; the mark not at 4 but at 3; the Swiss franc not at 4.30 but at 2.75; and so forth. If a German could buy a dollar for just 3 marks instead of 4, in essence this represented a markdown of 25 percent in the cost of any goods produced in the United States. Our exports would soar; our trade balance would begin correcting itself. Conversely, and more important, it meant that Americans would now see the cost of foreign products marked *up* by that same proportion when they tried to use dollars to buy a Volkswagen or a Sony TV, and would go back to purchasing American-made products.

The rest of the world flatly refused to go along with this. From their point of view, they at last had the United States on the run in economic terms. They had finally recovered from World War II to the point where they not only were able to surpass the Americans in steel and automobiles and consumer electronic products in *world* markets, but were now even able to hurdle American tariff barriers and increasingly penetrate that heretofore impregnable *home* market of the United States, the largest single market on earth. Why should they throw away this new-found competitive edge by revaluing their currencies?

Nixon sent Secretary of the Treasury John Connally, the ex-governor of Texas, to Rome to meet with all of Europe's finance ministers and bully them into it. Connally threatened them with everything short of a nuclear strike. They laughed at him. "The markets, not we," they said, "will now set the value of the dollar," and then sent him packing. His empty-handed departure temporarily marked the end of America's postwar economic imperialism, the end of a world in which the dollar had been king.

On the surface the world had now entered the era of freely floating exchange rates where the relationships of the dollar to the yen, the yen to the mark, the mark to the franc were now to be governed by supply and demand. As with other commodities, free-market forces would now also determine currencies' relative values. Right? Wrong! Because what the world was now really entering was the period of the "dirty" float. To prevent the dollar from falling to the level sought by the Americans, a level at which the American competitive position in international markets could be restored, central banks around the world began rigging the foreign-exchange markets by constantly buying up excess dollars. Such dollar-price-propping proved more difficult than most of them had anticipated. For there was now a massive outflow of money from the United States—stemming from private investors' fears of just that devaluation which Washington was unsuccessfully trying to engineer—meaning that the German, the Swiss, the Japanese central banks had to sop up immense numbers of dollars in order to maintain the dollar's high exchange value. For each dollar they absorbed, they had to give the seller counterpart funds in marks, francs and yen. Result: the whole world now started to create new money on a massive scale. In Japan and the seven European nations that carry a large influence in world financial matters, the average expansion in domestic money supply was 45 percent between year-end 1970 and mid-1973, a compound annual rate of nearly 16 percent a year!

The inflation that followed in all of these countries in 1973 and 1974 was obviously fueled by this huge wave of money creation.

Thus, where inflation was concerned, the U.S. had spread the virus to Europe and Japan.

This same virus had already begun to seriously affect the health of financial markets in the United States. The stock market averages, the barometers of such health, had been climbing almost uninterruptedly during the Eisenhower and Kennedy years and had even kept rising during the initial years of the Johnson presidency. The Dow Jones Industrial Average went from the 300 range in 1953 to the 1,000 mark during the first days of 1966. But when it became apparent on Wall Street that Johnson was not going to finance the Vietnam War and the Great Society on a pay-as-you-go basis, but rather through fiscal and monetary expansion (a process which, it was felt, would seriously undermine the basic functioning of the American economy), that bull market ended.

Nixon, through his suspension of dollar/gold convertibility in 1971, confirmed that his Administration considered the harm done by Johnson to be irreversible. The stock market reacted by meandering between 750 and that 1,000 mark for the entire *decade* that followed. It was not until 1982, after it became apparent that the Reagan/Volcker combination was determined to wring inflation out of the system at whatever cost in terms of unemployment, that the stage was set for the development of a new major bull market on Wall Street. In August of that year the stock market took off again and finally proceeded to move decisively through the 1,000 barrier.

Thus, once again, it was major economic events—one which became apparent in early 1966, the next which occurred in the summer of 1971, and the most recent which developed in 1981–82—that had watershed consequences for the direction the stock market would take.

Returning now to those fateful years of the early 1970's, what happened next was that OPEC hit the industrialized world with the oil embargo. Overnight the attitudes of foreign governments regarding dollar devaluation changed. If heretofore it had been in their interests to *prevent* it, now their self-interest lay in *promoting* it. Why? For the same reason: to protect their international competitive position relative to the United States. Energy costs are key to that, and one way to lessen the blow being dealt them by the Arabs was to compensate for the increase in the cost of oil by decreasing the cost of the dollar. For oil is a dollar commodity. Seen from inside Germany, when oil was $5 a barrel and the mark/dollar relationship was four to one, the deutsche mark cost of oil was DM 20.

Now that oil was $10 a barrel, the domestic cost of oil in Germany could
be held constant if the exchange value of the dollar was halved. At 2
deutsche marks per dollar, that $10-a-barrel oil would still cost DM 20 in
Germany. So instead of buying dollars, the Europeans and Japanese
started to sell them. At last a massive dollar devaluation resulted. The
Swiss franc rose from 4.30 to the dollar all the way up to 1.50; the mark
went from 4 to 1.75; the yen from 360 to 200. Then, with the ebb and
flow of money creation, these exchange rates started to gyrate in an
unprecedented manner. Sometimes the dollar/Swiss franc rate would
change more in one *hour* than it had over two previous *decades*.

The investment consequences of the oil embargo of 1973 were obvious
where the foreign-exchange markets were concerned: it was time to short
the dollar and go long on the currencies of the key non-oil-producing
industrialized countries, particularly Germany, Switzerland and Japan.

It was also time to invest in the stocks of the major international oil
companies. Sharply rising oil prices *had* to produce windfall profits for
these corporations, so the prices of their shares *had* to go up no matter
what the market as a whole might be doing. In fact, I think you can safely
generalize on the oil price/stock price relationship: oil price up, Exxon up.
As many investors in oil stocks found out in 1982–83, the reverse is also
true. When oil prices fall, so do the prices of oil company shares. Thus
about the only major industry group that was going steadily downhill while
the entire stock market was going up after August 1982 was the oils, since
it was during this same period that the price of crude oil dropped from
$34 to $29 a barrel, bringing oil companies' profits, and thus the value of
their shares, right down with it.

The oil embargo had one more very important investment consequence: by triggering a worldwide inflation it set the stage for two of the
most dramatic investment processes of recent times—the flights from
paper money into gold and real estate which occurred in the second half
of the 1970's.

All this shows that once again it was a unique major *economic* event
—the oil embargo of 1973—which opened up unique investment opportunities. Anybody who grasped the financial significance of the embargo,
and who then thought through—thought all the way through—what the
investment consequences would be, ended up making a lot of money in
the 1970's.

The point of all this history is that once the need for *monetary* discipline had disappeared along with the fixed-exchange-rate system set up
under the Bretton Woods arrangement, it gradually began to sink in that

there was also no longer any necessity for *fiscal* discipline, though it would take a while for us to reach that conclusion. Paradoxically, it was Ronald Reagan who first saw the opportunity and who then drove the third nail into that financial coffin in which we may eventually be buried. Because it was he and his people who came up with the concept of the "structural" deficit. And what, you may ask, is that? It is a deficit that has nothing to do with the ups and downs of the business cycle; it also has nothing to do with the Keynesian concept of priming the pump during recessions by creating demand through deficit spending. No, this doctrine states that deficits are now a *permanent* part of our economic system and—that's it, folks. Love 'em or—well, there is no leave 'em, since no matter where you might want to leave *for*, when you get there you are going to find exactly the same state of affairs you thought you had left behind.

Let's examine more closely this so-called structural deficit. As I have said, repeatedly, it really amounts to nothing more or less than the loss of the ability of governments of even the most highly developed countries on earth to pay their own way. This began to become evident in the United States during the Carter years, but really first sank in under his successor, a man devoted to balanced budgets if there ever was one. But under Ronald Reagan, for all his fiscal conservatism, the United States began piling up debts at an absolutely astounding rate. Reagan's deficits *started* at $110 billion in 1982, rose above $200 billion in 1983 and seem bound to remain in the $200 billion range indefinitely. But he insists that these deficits are no longer related to the business cycle. Instead they are built into the very system and thus, somehow or other, they are natural. Thus it came to pass that the conservative Lawrence Kudlow, when he was chief economist at the White House Office of Management and Budget and a key adviser to the fiscally ultraconservative Ronald Reagan, declared the following: Even *if* the American economy were to start to grow at 3 percent a year after inflation, and even *if* unemployment were to fall to 6 percent of the labor force, the deficit in fiscal 1988 would still be about $150 billion!

Kudlow's conclusion: "The chances of getting stable monetary policy, falling prices, and steady ready growth are very, very low." He could have added that with floating exchange rates, such chances approach nil.

Dr. Martin Feldstein, chairman of the President's Council of Economic Advisers, agrees with Kudlow's analysis. Feldstein says that the "cyclical" part of the deficit will diminish as economic growth continues in 1984 and perhaps beyond. But, he points out, the structural deficit is forecast to grow as rapidly as the cyclical deficit shrinks because future spending increases will exceed future rises in tax revenue. Dr. Feldstein's conclusion: "By 1988, the entire projected budget deficit [of about $210 billion] is structural."

Well, we will want to keep these words in mind later on in this book because they certainly will affect how we plan our future investments. For what Kudlow and Feldstein are in essence telling us is this: since government borrowings are going to *have to stay very high for a very long time even under the best of conditions,* you can say goodbye to low interest rates for the rest of this decade and who knows how long thereafter? Translated into investment terms, this means that current holders of bonds, like yesterday's investors in diamonds, are going to find out that no investment is forever. Of course a lot of Americans already know this, the ones who put their life's savings into municipals at the beginning of the 1970's, for as interest rates moved higher and higher, the value of their bonds fell ever lower, with the result that at the end of the seventies they had lost half their money. This process culminated in the monetary crisis evoked by Paul Volcker in 1981. By starving the money markets, the Fed drove long-term interest rates to levels never before seen here in this century.

The turning point occurred in 1982. Volcker's credit crunch broke the back of the economy, and the nation plunged into deep recession; interest rates also plunged as the borrowing needs of the private sector collapsed along with the economy. The inevitable result: between the end of June 1982 and the end of November 1982, bond prices *rose* 35 percent! This was like being in silver when Bunker Hunt was trying to corner the market. To be sure, bonds subsequently began to cool off as interest rates leveled, but, in contrast to silver of yesteryear, their price levels sustained themselves and they remained good investments. But for how long this time? Will bonds turn sour once again in the 1980's just as they did in the 1970's? Most probably yes.

High bond prices can only be sustained indefinitely if, in Kudlow's words, we have "stable monetary policies, falling prices, and steady ready growth" in the future. He says we won't, so if Kudlow is right, bond prices can't. As simple as that. For there is no magic whatsoever where bond prices are concerned. They move in the opposite direction to interest rates. Interest up, bonds down. Period.

Though bonds are good investments in the short term if interest rates are static or falling, they are a risky long-term bet. The main reason, and this same reason applies equally to Belgian, Danish and British bonds, is that during the past ten years governmental expenditures related to social programs, especially entitlements involving benefit payments to individuals whether they need them or not, have exploded in volume and are now out of control. In the United States these outlays take the form of food stamps, Medicare, federal employee pensions and all kinds of support programs for everybody from unwed mothers to students who have no mothers. I have two friends, each of whom has a net worth of over $10 million, whose kids get $500 a month from the government to help them get through college . . . because in both cases their mothers had died when the children were small. Both men tried to stop the payments: neither succeeded. The fiscal Frankenstein's monster that threatens us is even better exemplified by the American Social Security system. The average American will pay in about $7,500 to Social Security in his lifetime, and some of those same average Americans will get as much as *fifty* times that amount back before they die. Ditto for the average German, Swiss and Swede. But that's just the beginning. This average American and Swiss and Swede also expects to get unemployment insurance forever if his job runs out; he expects the doctors and hospitals to take care of him indefinitely if he gets chronically ill; he expects his 2.7 children to be put through college at government expense if he cannot afford to support them. Why does he expect all this? Because his government said he *should*. The *law* says he is *entitled* to such things. We have, in the words of some cynic, essentially granted lifetime tenure to the underprivileged.

But where the hell is the money going to come from to provide all this? Why didn't anybody anticipate that we simply could not afford to supply ourselves with these programs when they were first put into place?

Because when most of these programs were started in the second half of the 1960's and the early 1970's, the solution was easy and clear: *growth*. We, the whole world, were going to keep increasing our collective wealth at the rate of 4 or 5 percent a year in the future just as we had been doing, more or less, since the end of the war. Under such conditions, if every working person just chipped in a few percentage points of his ever-increasing income, the needs of everybody else could be taken care of. What was so terrific was that the percentage would really never have to change even if the size and breadth of the welfare programs did—as they were all scheduled to do. Anybody could figure out that if income doubled every ten or twelve years, the amounts available for welfare would likewise double even if the percentage of income that we had to "transfer" to the "needy" stayed exactly the same.

A wonderful theory, but it hasn't worked out that way. As we have already seen, growth was stopped dead in its tracks by the first oil shock in 1973; stopped again in 1979 by the second oil shock; stopped yet again by the monetary shock of 1981. But despite the fact that the overall economy was becoming increasingly stagnant, the welfare programs went on and on, growing ever larger, eating up ever-rising percentages of governments' available resources.

How much more are we talking about? In the United States, spending for social programs was 1 percent of the entire federal budget in 1950. In 1983 it was 26 percent. In real numbers this comes out to $190 billion now vs. $1.5 billion then, and we're supposed to be the last country to hang on to "primitive" capitalism with its basic "sink or swim" attitude toward the individual. The explosion in the cost of social programs which occurred simultaneously in Western Europe was even greater, despite the fact that in most cases the Europeans started from a much higher historical base.

How to finance all this? Since throughout the West the overall economies were growing less and less, what was done—the world over—was to increase taxation, i.e., increase that percentage "bite" that we had all been told would stay more or less the same forever. Put another way, governments had to "preempt" an ever larger proportion of national income, of increments in national wealth, to pay for the growth of social expenditures which nobody could stop. In other words, governments began to tax the hell out of their working citizens.

Some examples: the ratio of taxes to the value of the country's output (gross domestic product)—the percentage bite—in Sweden went from 25.5 percent in 1955 to 50 percent in 1980. In Norway it went from 28 percent in 1955 to 47 percent in 1980 (and this in a country that struck it rich in oil in the North Sea during the same period); in the Netherlands from 26 percent to 46 percent. I cite these particular cases since these countries were the pioneers in expanding the government's role in the overall economy by assuming responsibility for everything from stimulating growth to redistributing income to guaranteeing income and jobs. They may very well represent the future that still awaits a lot of the rest of us. Not that that future is so far off, however.

This government "takeover" which started in Scandinavia in the 1950's began to occur in earnest in the rest of the developed world a decade later. Since 1965 the percentage of total national output preempted by government to pay for its expenditures has increased by 10 percent in every major country in Europe, including such "models" of restraint as Germany and Switzerland. Japan and Canada have done the same. In Belgium and Luxembourg, government has increased its grab of the entire nation's annual creation of new wealth by over 15 percent during the same period.

↳ major disincentive

The result is that in every major country in Europe today, government now taxes and spends at least 40 percent of total national income. If you take all of North America, Western Europe and Japan combined (the area of the Organization for Economic Cooperation and Development), the tax ratio has gone from 24.7 percent in 1955 to over 37 percent today.

So what?

The answer was provided forty years ago by one of this century's great economists, the Australian Colin Clark. He had already advanced the theory that whenever a country's tax ratio exceeds 25 percent, inflation becomes inevitable. In the 1970's the empirical evidence for this was provided in country after country, as we have seen in Chapter 4, when rates of inflation reached record heights around the world and then went through ever more violent gyrations.

It might have taken forty years for this truth to sink in, but it finally did at the end of the 1970's, when governments collectively concluded that the limits of taxation had been reached. If tax ratios of 25 percent produced inflation, tax rates of 55 percent would probably produce hyperinflation. Governments likewise began to realize that to seek to collect yet more to pay for still rising expenditures would be counterproductive in another very important sense: higher tax rates would so reduce the incentive to earn more that they would lead to the perverse situation where the tax base might actually begin to shrink: individuals would begin substituting leisure for work, they would consume rather than save, they would increasingly join the underground economy; they would start to cheat on their taxes in a truly major fashion. So to seek a bigger slice of a now shrinking pie through higher tax *rates* would result in lower overall tax *revenue*, i.e., in a net *loss* in government income.

That, by the way, is all—absolutely all—that the now famous Laffer curve is about, a curve supposedly drawn on the back of a napkin by a curly-haired young professor of economics from southern California, one who also predicted, by the way, that the United States would return to a gold standard before the end of 1982. But back to the curve. Supposedly Ronald Reagan gazed upon it and at once became convinced that should he *cut* tax rates, instead of raising them as all his immediate predecessors had done, this would remove an important barrier to economic growth. America would soon prosper. Tax receipts would swell as income surged, and Good Times would be just around the corner. Many scoffed when Reagan implemented just such tax-rate reductions at the beginning of this Administration, only to see the American economy sink into the deepest recession since the 1930's. But then in 1983 recovery *did* set in. Incomes *did* start to rise. Maybe Laffer and Reagan were right. Maybe the tax cuts *were* now gradually becoming effective as a growth stimulus. The trouble was that the deficit, instead of disappearing, confounded everyone by continuing to grow ever larger. For the anticipated increases in tax receipts as the recovery progressed had at first been nonexistent, and then were so slow in coming that they by no means compensated for the inexorable, rapid, continuing rise in expenditures. What the Laffer/Reagan experiment seems to have demonstrated, at least thus far, is that nowadays you are damned if you tax and damned if you don't tax. The outcome in either case will be larger deficits.

To restate the problem:

a. By the beginning of the 1980's, social programs were in place throughout the world in the form of legal promises to provide ever more lavish social benefits to the citizenry. All industrialized countries

b. No government could reverse such promises and survive.

c. Although we have not discussed it yet, an immense acceleration in defense spending was under way, especially in the United States— expenditure increases which were considered just as acutely necessary as those related to the entitlements programs.

d. By the beginning of the 1980's the levels of taxation had reached such heights that to increase them further to cover these now *automatically* rising government expenses was no longer a way out, since it would be ultimately counterproductive.

So what do you do?

If you can't tax, and you've got to pay, then you borrow. In fact you *must* borrow. Because the consequences for Western democracies of not doing so to maintain the "benefit" system would be devastating. Peter Peterson, formerly Secretary of Commerce of the United States under Mr. Nixon, has been perhaps the best informed of the "independent" thinkers on this subject. The fact that he was chairman of the board of Lehman Brothers Kuhn Loeb, one of the nation's most prestigious investment banks, and is now running his own venture capital firm, may make him slightly suspect where considerations of the poor and needy are concerned; but even if that were not so, Peterson, as an investment banker, knows that if the "system" goes, he goes. And that is in essence the conclusion he has reached.

"To put the matter bluntly," he wrote in the the *New York Review of*

Books, "Social Security is headed for a crash. We cannot permit this to happen, because it would put the nation itself in serious jeopardy. Though in effect for only two generations, Social Security has become the defining link between citizen and state in modern America. It has such uniform and reverential support that if the system crashes, so almost certainly will civic harmony and the economy itself."

Peterson has called this the dullest subject in the universe, and he is probably right, but things can be both dull and lethal, like famines. "The only alternative to reorganizing Social Security," he writes, "is to sit by while the system collapses, either through an ugly revolt of young taxpaying workers against their elders or through a catastrophic flood of deficits."

The problem facing us is essentially two-fold: the Social Security Insurance System (providing old age and survivor benefits) and the Medicare program, which was later integrated into the overall Social Security system. Contrary to all the fears raised at the beginning of this decade, the program involving old-age benefits is *not* going to collapse in our generation, and frankly, what happens in the year 2010 doesn't particularly bother or even interest me. I'm worried about the next three, five, ten years.

The immediate real danger which the recent "crisis" regarding the Social Security System latently presented was that the "bailout" was going to take the form mostly of an infusion of massive amounts of funding from general revenues, i.e., from tax receipts that are not there, meaning that the Old-Age and Survivors Insurance trust fund would have had to be financed by additional massive borrowings by the government. To avert this crisis, Alan Greenspan and President Reagan and Tip O'Neill came up with a solution in early 1983 which does *not* require such a massive infusion and thus such massive additional borrowings. A mixture of minor downward adjustments in benefits and equally minor upward adjustments in Social Security payroll taxes, plus somewhat expanded coverage, means that the insurance system will stay viable through this decade, and well beyond, on its own. Specifically, the trustees of the system now estimate that the Social Security trust fund will be in the *black* to the tune of $123.5 billion by 1990.

To be sure, everyone does not share the trustees' optimism regarding the future solvency of the Old-Age fund. They point out that the Greenspan formula will work only if this country once again enjoys reasonably high sustained growth. If the economy falls apart, and payroll taxes begin to fall below the Greenspan projections, then the Social Security trust fund will go bust.

But even if the Greenspan formula works and future retirement benefits will now be amply covered, *half* the problem remains unsolved. For as Peterson now stresses, it is the *other totally unfunded* commitments of government that are going to raise future havoc, and in many cases that future is soon. Medicare, which, of course, is now also part of the overall Social Security system, is the most worrisome of the programs involving such immense unfunded commitments. The trustees of the Medicare trust fund have themselves bluntly stated that by 1990 that fund will be fully depleted. Yet the system will still be committed to making health benefit payments approaching $100 billion annually. By 1994 the cumulative shortfall in the Medicare program will have risen to $400 billion.

Another problem is this nation's promise to provide huge disability benefits. Retirement plans for state and municipal workers in the United States are already short $200 billion of the amounts committed in future payments. Old-age plans for federal personnel are underfunded by $1 *trillion.* The military system alone has future pension liabilities of $477 billion, and to this day remains totally unfunded.

Social programs are immediately dangerous where our common economic future is concerned only if they must be funded from general revenue during times when such revenue is no longer available . . . like now, when to fund means to borrow. Social Sec. should come from what we saved.

For to repeat it once more, governments today realize that the limits of taxation have more or less been reached given current economic parameters. Thus there is little chance that any government is going to attempt to soak the young to calm the old and risk an "ugly revolt." Likewise, no government could survive a deliberate "breach of social contract" with its ex-employees, nor with the military, where their pensions are concerned; nor with the poor where their food stamps are concerned; nor with the middle class where their kids' educations are concerned; nor with the old or unemployed where health care is concerned.

So we are back to the same conclusion: if you've got to pay and you can't tax, you are simply going to have to borrow.

How much?

The biggest fiscal entity on earth, the United States government, is going to have to borrow appreciably more money during the 1980's than it did during the entire prior two hundred years of its existence. On top of the social programs component of the U.S. budget, which seems to be essentially irreducible, the two other major components, namely military spending and interest costs, seem equally so. The United States has in place an eight-year $2 trillion military program designed to "modernize" its military establishment, meaning that old weapons systems are going to be progressively replaced by new ones—the new involving everything from MX and cruise missiles to the B-1 bomber to the enormously expensive M-1 Abrams tank to the $32 billion program to launch a new generation of Navy cruisers of the Aegis type. Cost analysts in the Pentagon know, and have repeatedly stated semi-publicly, that this figure is well below the real cost that can be expected. In that context, the continuing debate between Congress and the Administration, and the resulting recurring promises by Defense Secretary Caspar Weinberger to pare $10 billion here and maybe $20 billion there, are meaningless. That portion of the $2 trillion which, at least initially, could have been substantially reduced—through the elimination of the development of overlapping weapons systems—is now irrevocably committed: it would be *more* expensive to turn back.

Not that there is any intention in either the White House or the Pentagon of turning back in any case. For just as the current Administration seeks "restoration" of America's globally dominant economic position through the application of supply-side theories, it likewise seeks the restoration of American global military preeminence through rapid, massive rearmament. Put simplistically but I think realistically, the grand design envisions a restoration of the 1950's under Eisenhower in the 1980's under Reagan.

Is such a thing feasible?

Of course not. Not only is it not feasible, but the confrontational attitude vis-à-vis the Soviet Union which is part and parcel of that grand design has raised the risk of war, and is increasingly alienating the populations of the key members of our last remaining alliance, NATO. The result could well be exactly the opposite of what we enjoyed in the 1950's because the Europeans may eventually choose to "opt out" from in between. The idea that the Russians and Americans will fight to the last European does not particularly appeal to them. But the United States cannot opt out. Without Europe it would face a painful reformulation of its defense posture, and probably end up becoming an "island nation" with its defense firepower concentrated in the Western hemisphere and on the world's oceans. In any case, given the progressively weakening resolve of our remaining allies, plus the fact that most of them find themselves facing even greater economic difficulties than America faces, it seems likely that at the end of the 1980's the United States is going to be burdened with an even higher proportion of the cost of defending the West than it is today.

To be sure, this is based upon the perhaps fragile assumption that hardliners are going to remain in the White House through most of the rest of the 1980's. Another assumption is that the Kremlin will continue to be run by men who hope to make Russia the global equivalent of Hertz as far as relative military strength is concerned, while the United States becomes Avis. It is precisely this analogy that was used by a leading Soviet official in a conversation I recently had with him. The conversation ended with his suggesting that tensions could be greatly reduced if I—we—started to get used to the idea.

To put it mildly, such a Soviet intent for a reversal of the military status of the two superpowers, if indeed it exists, is hardly compatible with the Reagan strategy for restoration of America's strategic superiority, for *both* now insist upon being Hertz.

So as much as one hopes that "good guys," seeing the folly of the nuclear arms race, will someday simultaneously rise to power in both Washington and Moscow and "work things out," the chance that that will happen soon seems rather remote, although impossible it is not. Who would have believed that two hardliners like Nixon and Mao could have struck a deal within a remarkably short time, ending almost overnight what had amounted to a perpetual state of undeclared war between the American and Chinese nations?

How nice it would be if the undeclared war between the Soviet Union and the United States could end with another such flourish, and with it the need for such huge arsenals. But unfortunately the foreign policy and military establishments in both nations remain convinced that the need for a maximum deterrent seems hardly less today than it was twenty years ago, or forty years ago. In American eyes Russia remains true to its nineteenth-century tradition as an expansionistic power. In the words of President Reagan, the Soviet Union is "the focus of evil in the modern world." To be sure, nobody really believes that the Red Army is going to attack Berlin. But there can be no doubt that the majority of those in power in the United States believe, and probably correctly so, that the main thrust of the Soviets is to get us out of Europe through *political* means, playing precisely on those growing European fears of American trigger-happiness where nuclear weapons are concerned. And it is not just American observers who have reached this conclusion. André Fontaine recently wrote this in *Le Monde:*

Experience unfortunately shows that when dealing with interlocutors as stubborn as the Soviets, unilateral disarmament measures have rarely produced reciprocal gestures. Jimmy Carter abandoned the neutron bomb, the B-1 bomber and suspended the manufacture of ICBM's. The Kremlin reacted by deploying SS-20's. Why? It is obviously not to grab Western Europe by force of arms; once atom-bombed, of what use is it? The idea is to scare the Europeans sufficiently to convince them that the best way to avoid being hit by lightning is not to have a lightning rod.

The Soviet perception of us is that we have "encircled" them; that the intention of the United States is to tighten the noose, driving Russia into ever deeper isolation; that should the Americans ever conclude that *their* hegemony of the West was endangered (by, say, a Soviet challenge, real or imagined, in the Middle East), they would not hesitate to introduce the use of nuclear weapons to defend the oil fields, since the Americans themselves have stated that they lack the ability to defend them by conventional means. Next stage: nuclear first strikes against the Soviet Union proper. That, they say, is why we insist on the MX and the Pershing II, both first-strike missiles.

Paranoid as much of this sounds, the fact remains that both sides remain convinced that they have no choice but to remain highly armed as a deterrent.

But even *if* the highly unlikely occurred, *if* both sides decided to lessen their dependence on the nuclear deterrent and began to increase their dependence on nonnuclear weapons, the net result in financial terms would be a *major increase* in defense costs. The new strategy, under which nuclear weapons would be used only as the last resort instead of in the first days or even hours of a Soviet/American conflict, would require a move toward a "forward defense" posture in Europe, meaning that NATO Europe would be defended at the East German border. It would be defended there with "deep strike" nonnuclear defense devices, meaning long-range conventional weapons that could detect and destroy Warsaw Pact forces up to two hundred miles behind the new front line. To develop and deploy such new systems, to move American forces in Germany from the Rhine-Main area where they are now concentrated to the East German frontier (involving implementation of the so-called "Master Restationing Plan"), would cost tens upon tens of billions of *additional* defense dollars. Uncle Sam would end up providing most of them.

Given current political and military realities, we would be kidding ourselves if we hoped that financial salvation lies in halving the defense budget. In fact, I think that despite the rhetoric, there is an overwhelming consensus in Washington that something very close to that $2 trillion must and will be spent in the end. So this part of the budget is just as irreducible a future expense item as are entitlements.

Where interest costs are concerned, the good news is that the average rate of interest on the national debt of more than $1.4 trillion has stabilized, at least temporarily, in the 10 percent range as a result of generally falling interest rates during the past couple of years. The bad news is that the U.S. federal debt, which was less than a trillion dollars at the beginning of the decade, will exceed $2 trillion well before it ends. Thus during this decade interest costs will double, adding, in the process, still more to the size of the gap that must be filled by still more borrowing, which will cost still more interest, which will require still more borrowing. The United States, in other words, has become its own Brazil.

Where the ultimate borrowing needs of the American government are concerned, the grand total in any given year will always be appreciably higher than the budgetary deficit itself—due to the so-called off-budget items. These include borrowing to finance the rural electrification programs and the purchase of crude oil for the strategic petroleum reserve, and borrowing by such federally sponsored agencies as the Federal National Mortgage Association. These off-budget items add another $10 billion to $15 billion each year to the new cash needs of Uncle Sam, cash requirements which will be met before anybody else gets a crack at the pool of lendable funds available in the nation's—in the world's—credit markets. By 1983 federal borrowing already represented 45 percent of the net borrowing in U.S. credit markets. In fiscal 1984 federal borrowing will absorb 94 percent of this nation's private savings, this according to the Reagan Administration's own calculations. What's going to be left over for General Motors or New York City or you and me? Damn little, that's what.

Now, what is true for the United States is at least as true for the rest of the world where the cost of domestic programs is concerned. In fact, if you consider only entitlements and the inability of governments to cover their costs through taxation, America is essentially still a laggard *falling behind*, relative to Western Europe, Canada and Australia. My calculations indicate that during the next five years, on average, in the absence of very high rates of sustained overall economic growth throughout the highly industrialized world, central governments will have to borrow the following amounts each and every year:

· The United States will need at least $200 billion annually.
· The German government will need almost $20 billion.
· Italy will need $55 billion.
· France will need $30 billion.
· Benelux will need $20 billion.
· Scandinavia will need $20 billion.
· Japan will need $55 billion.
· The Canadian government will have to borrow $30 billion.
· The lesser developed countries without oil will need $50 billion.
· Eastern Europe will need $15 billion.
· The United Kingdom, paradoxically, has one of the world's smallest public-sector borrowing requirements, in the range of $12 billion a year, the result of murderous taxation and North Sea oil.

It may be surprising to learn that OPEC members—yes, OPEC!—will need somewhere between $25 billion and $50 billion a year because of a key and totally unexpected shift in the global flow of funds. During the past decade, the biggest generator of savings for the rest of the world was OPEC, probably $450 billion in all. It was the low-population OPEC nations—Saudi Arabia, Kuwait, the Emirates—that chiefly generated those savings, which, as we have seen, the banks borrowed and then lent to the LDCs. *Now* not only will OPEC members not be generating any more net savings, but, as a result of the new oil shock—a "reverse" shock where this time it is the Arabs who are on the receiving end—they are going to have to *dissave* on a massive scale. All have enormous development programs in place and all these programs were geared to projected oil income based on OPEC production at a minimum level of 30 million barrels a day, to be sold at a minimum price of $34 a barrel. With output now at less than two thirds of this level, and with prices substantially lower than anticipated, in order to keep only the most important of such programs going ("important" insofar as they help the moderate Arab regimes maintain domestic political tranquility), the Arabs will have to withdraw probably as much as $50 billion a year from the Western financial system. This $500 billion turnaround in the flow of funds between us and them will add heavily to the potential shortage of capital available in the world.

If you throw in Australia and Greece and Portugal and Finland and Spain, among others, you easily get well beyond $600 billion annual net new borrowing by the world's central governments. No states, no cantons, no cities are included. Yet it would be unrealistic to think that Milan and

Frankfurt and the province of Ontario and even the canton of Zurich are not going to have to borrow, and borrow massively, in the years immediately ahead.

How will these governments raise the money? Well, here is where we start moving from the present to the future. The answer to this question represents probably the key to the formulation of individual financial strategies for coping with the economic future.

Part II

○◎○○○◎○○○◎○○○◎○○○◎○○◎○

The Future

Chapter 8

o◉oo◉oo◉o

The Road Back to Inflation?

JACQUES DE LAROSIÈRE DE CHAMPFEU is the managing director of the International Monetary Fund. The *Wall Street Journal* calls him a "tough guy." But he is also a Frenchman with a sense of humor, somewhat of a rarity at least among that country's senior bureaucrats, particularly when they are forced to deal with Americans, who are generally regarded in their circles as subhuman. The *Journal* also says of him that he is "an accomplished horseman, skier, and trout fisherman, and still retains a luxurious Paris apartment and several country homes in France," which would indicate that he is hardly just a civil servant in search of a tax-free income at the IMF. He had been chief of staff to Valéry Giscard d'Estaing when Giscard was France's finance minister. Then de Larosière moved on to become the French counterpart of the U.S. Secretary of the Treasury for Monetary Affairs.

Since his appointment to the IMF in 1978 he has emerged as the first truly global central banker. When he talks it pays to listen. In speech after speech he has focused on government deficits and has repeatedly warned of the serious consequences that may face all of us unless the gap between outgoings and incomings can be drastically narrowed. It was he who pointed out that there are three ways, and only three ways, that these huge governmental deficits can be funded. Through:

1. Foreign borrowing
2. Domestic borrowing *without* monetary expansion
3. Domestic borrowing *with* monetary expansion

Some bankers, like Walter Wriston of Citibank, seem to think that it is unnecessary to worry about such matters. Disaster is not inevitable. "To see why," Wriston wrote in the New York *Times*, "it is only necessary to understand the basic facts of government borrowing. The first is that there are few recorded instances in history of government—any government—actually getting out of debt." If I had lent 146 percent of my bank's capital and reserves to the governments of Mexico, Venezuela and Brazil, I would no doubt be saying the same thing.

The more probable truth is that government borrowing in any form—after it has reached a certain percentage of total funds borrowed in a nation's capital market (such as the 45 percent rate today in the United States, as compared to the average federal participation rate in the domestic credit market of 20 percent during the past quarter-century) becomes dangerous and, in fact, becomes the *chief* danger in your economic future and mine. Furthermore, each *type* of borrowing—and remember there are only three ways that any government can go—sows its own seeds of future destruction.

The way to get into *real* trouble quickly is to take the first route and rely on foreign borrowing, as Mexico did. What the Mexican case demonstrates is that when a nation suddenly finds it can no longer function in the world economy without further new loans, its government has little choice but to put the country into the hands of foreign interests. The alternative of going all the way into de jure default is hardly a realistic one, since any nation that tries it will find itself cast into financial outer darkness forevermore, its assets abroad subject to seizure at any time. Thus Mexico's economic policies are now determined by the staff of the International Monetary Fund's office in Washington with the not-so-tacit assistance of Mexico's nervous bankers in New York and London and Tokyo. The result can be summed up in one word—austerity. In 1983 Mexico experienced the worst recession it had seen in forty years, and this in a country where 40 percent of the labor force was already either unemployed or underemployed.

Next in line for the same treatment was Brazil. But there acquiescence to the demands of the bankers had already proved more difficult. Symptomatic was a Brazilian cartoon depicting the International Monetary Fund as a bloodthirsty ogre devouring the children of the world while their parents fall in line behind the Stars and Stripes. Brazil, the critics in São Paulo claimed, was selling its soul to the devil . . . in the form of the IMF, the secular arm of North America. In the end the Brazilian government accepted the dictates of the Monetary Fund by breaking the index-linking of wages to prices, a move designed to reverse the inflationary spiral and restore Brazil's competitive position in the world, allowing it once again to *earn* enough dollars to service its debt. The result, however, will be a 20 percent cut in real wages in Brazil, in a country where the majority of workers earn less than $80 a month and where 49 percent of all families live below the poverty line. Such is the price that Brazil must now pay for continuing to expand its economy in 1979–81 despite the slowdown in the rest of the world and borrowing frantically from the banks of the industrialized world to meet the ensuing current account deficits.

However, it is not just the poor underdeveloped nations that get themselves into such messes. For a while the United States was heading into the same kind of trouble. A few years ago I wrote a novel called *The Crash of '79*, in which the Arabs began withdrawing vast amounts of money that they had invested in United States government securities and deposited with American commercial banks—causing a financial panic in New York and ultimately bringing about an old-fashioned "crash." It didn't quite work out that way in '79, but we came close on at least two occasions.

In real life during the 1970's the Arabs, particularly the Saudis and the Kuwaitis, had indeed amassed a huge portfolio of U.S. Treasury bills and notes and bonds involving tens of billions of dollars. The result was that they were all of a sudden the biggest single *foreign* source of financing for the steadily rising debt of the United States. Furthermore, as we have already seen, they were simultaneously depositing huge sums with the American money center banks, banks which, in turn, are the largest *domestic* purchasers of the debt paper issued by the U.S. government.

The late congressman Benjamin Rosenthal began to worry about this exposure and held extensive hearings in July 1979 trying to determine exactly how vulnerable as a nation we really were to such foreign financial interests. The Treasury officials refused to tell him, since for years they have had a "deal" with the Arabs under which our government won't reveal how much any given country in the Middle East has of our debt, provided it keeps accumulating it. Another government agency, the General Accounting Office, testified that it really didn't matter how much the Arabs had here in the form of government securities or anything else, since they had no choice but to keep it here. There was no currency, in the final analysis, they claimed, in which the funds could be kept except dollars. And the only place dollars could ultimately be held was at American banks. So why worry the American people unnecessarily, they said, about a "problem" that was really just a monetary mirage.

It was almost unbelievable, when you think of it: in essence the executive branch of our government was telling the legislative branch to stop rocking the Treasury's boat—that all this was really not fit for public consumption. Well, Rosenthal asked me to drop by the hearings, where I testified to the effect that since tens upon tens of billions of dollars were involved, and since they were eminently "yankable," and furthermore, since these dollars were also eminently *convertible* into marks or francs or yen, they represented a clear and present danger to our currency and to our financial system, and I gave an example.

In the final days of October 1978, I said, the following had happened: The dollar had been sinking all year, but it was hoped that in mid-October President Carter would finally come up with a coherent and effective anti-inflationary program for the United States. He did not, and more serious dumping of U.S. dollars began. When on the final day of that month word started to circulate around Wall Street that Kuwait had failed to renew an extremely large deposit with Morgan Guaranty—a figure between $1 billion and $2 billion was mentioned—the dumping that resulted resembled the start of a run on the currency. The *Wall Street Journal* a few days later stated that we were on the edge of "a 19th Century kind of financial panic from which a genuine depression could have resulted."

Fortunately, this panic was a "contained" one—affecting only the foreign-exchange markets. Had the Federal Reserve Bank of New York not stepped in at the last minute to stabilize the dollar, who knows what might have happened to the stock market, the bond market and even that untouchable, the market for U.S. government securities? What this near-miss shows is that in an increasingly complicated economic world, the risk exposure of the individual *American* investor has taken on global dimensions. That's why it pays to read the front page of your paper as well as the financial section. Increasingly it is those events developing on the front page on Monday which lead to the serious investment losses you first learn about in the financial section on Thursday—when it is too late to do anything about them.

One of the suggestions I made to Rosenthal was that in view of this near catastrophe, "contingency plans for coping with any possible large-scale withdrawal of funds from the U.S. and U.S. financial institutions should be drawn up *now* because once such a process starts, days and even hours are of the essence." I suggested that the best approach would be to prepare the papers allowing for immediate sequestration of a nation's funds, just as the United States had done with the funds of Iran in the fictional plot of *The Crash of '79*, a sequestration designed to counter the shah's threat to pull out of the dollar before he began blowing up the world.

Well, a year later the government of Iran actually did threaten exactly such a massive pullout of its funds. Within hours, in fact at five o'clock in the morning, President Carter signed the pre-prepared papers that provided for sequestering Iranian assets, and headed off a possible rerun of the October 1978 crisis.

I think Washington has learned its lesson regarding overreliance on foreign governments for funding the American debt. Today foreign holdings of U.S. Treasury notes and bonds—private and governmental—amount to less than $100 billion, or only around 7 percent of total government debt. The percentage in the hands of Middle Eastern governments is steadily diminishing as they must increasingly sell off their foreign investments to fill the financial gap being left by steadily lower oil income. This orderly withdrawal of Arab funds is creating no problems whatsoever for the United States, since we are able to minimize our reliance upon foreign financing of our deficits because we still have the world's largest and most viable capital market at home in New York.

But an increasing number of other nations have no choice. They must rely on foreign governments and private banks for capital. And I don't mean just the Brazils and Costa Ricas of the world. Some very highly developed nations of the West are today forced to finance an ever-larger percentage of their deficits by borrowing abroad. Denmark is a prime example. It has one of the world's highest standards of living; the government truly takes care of everybody from the cradle to the grave. To pay for this, Denmark runs budgetary deficits equal to 12 percent to 14 percent of the country's total output each and every year. How can Denmark's tiny capital market provide the funds necessary to finance such deficits? Answer: it can't. The Danish government drains off as much as it can from Denmark's capital market until, even when government kroner bonds yield 20 percent plus at times, there simply are no more takers. Then it is forced to go abroad, as it has done for years, to fund a rapidly rising proportion of the cost of its extraordinarily generous social welfare programs. Ten years ago Denmark owed the rest of the world only $2 billion. Today it already has an external debt of $18 billion. Next year this debt will rise to well over $20 billion. This is the price that Denmark, like the rest of Scandinavia, must pay for having pushed its tax ratio to the absolute limit . . . over 50 percent. The country's capacity to pay for further governmental programs is exhausted. Arthur Laffer should have been a Dane.

Belgium has done exactly the same thing. Today it owes at least $15 billion to foreign lenders. Or consider France. Under the new socialist regime of François Mitterrand, its external debt went from $28.7 billion to over $50 billion in two years. It was forced to make "deals" with such countries as Saudi Arabia, by which the Saudis agreed to deposit $4 billion in French banks in return for French governmental promises to provide them with military hardware—Exocets. Portugal owes $10 billion; Spain, $13 billion; Greece, $7 billion. In all cases their economies are stagnant and so are their tax receipts. But the cost of entitlements continues to rise.

Now, if such foreign debts were being accumulated in order to rebuild industry and commerce, to establish a more competitive national production base so that the country could export more and thus earn more dollars, these debts would in essence be self-liquidating. But what is involved here is quite the opposite: *these debts are being piled up to finance current consumption.* It's as if you mortgaged your house to buy gas for your car. Eventually you'd have no house and no gas either. Furthermore, when a government sops up all the money in sight at home, before it finally resorts to borrowing abroad, the cost of "local" money becomes so prohibitive that the private sector can afford to borrow less and less. Thus total private investment in Denmark has dropped from 25 percent of GNP at the beginning of the 1970's to 14 percent at the beginning of the 1980's. Denmark's plant and equipment are aging and deteriorating, for its productive future has been mortgaged to pay for today's consumption. As one of Denmark's bankers has put it: "We are on the way to hell, but we are doing it first class."

What Denmark and Belgium and France are essentially doing when they finance their domestic entitlements programs through foreign borrowings is exporting their problems. The funds that they absorb come from two sources: either the international long-term capital market (which they tap by issuing Eurobonds, normally denominated in U.S. dollars) or the huge multinational commercial banks, which join together in consortia sometimes involving as many as three hundred institutions for one loan.

But why does this mean that the Danes and the Belgians and the French are "exporting" their problems?

Because such loans divert capital from the *private sector* of the *rest* of the world, capital which ought to have been devoted to investment, the

font of all economic growth. Instead of investment for economic growth
—for roads or airports or to finance scientific research (end uses which
would certainly legitimize such borrowings)—governments are sopping up
these scarce capital funds and transferring them immediately to their
citizenry to pay for dental costs or vacations, or subsidizing farmers to feed
cows to produce milk to make butter which cannot possibly be sold due
to the global butter glut. In other words, what we have here is *dead-end
financing* amounting to a crass misuse of precious savings, savings which
their countries no longer generate because their citizens are already so
greatly overtaxed. So such governments and such countries are now going
after the savings of frugal Switzerland and Germany or those generated
by more productive America or Japan *at the expense of the citizenry of
these countries.* The well shut Gurus.

It is just such global financial trends—such large events, if you will—
which you must monitor if your personal investment planning is going to
prove effective. For the steady growth in the size of deficits, not just ours
but those of Denmark and Belgium and France as well, has reached such
a point today that investments in single-family houses in the United States
are to be avoided. Why? Because fewer and fewer Americans can afford
them. The demand that drove up the prices of houses in the 1970's—and
produced huge profits for investors who had speculated in real estate
during that period—has substantially disappeared in the 1980's. Why?
Because the cost of financing the purchase of a single-family dwelling is
simply out of the reach of most American families today. Why? Because
mortgage rates are now 13 or 14 percent instead of just 8 percent as they
were in 1975. Why? Because today governments (plural) need so much
money to finance their programs that they borrow well over half the
lendable funds available in dollars, instead of just the 20 percent they used
to, competing for money that used to be available for home mortgages and
driving up the price of that money and interest rates in general.

Ultimately, then, the fact that mortgage rates in California are at 13
or 14 percent, so that new houses go begging and our American overall
economic growth slows down accordingly, is partly the fault of the Den-
marks and Mexicos which have exported the costs of their profligate social
spending to us. So far they have no intention of reforming their ways, for
their politicians are as helpless as ours when it comes to taking back from
the voters what they are accustomed to getting. *completely given up to dissipation*

The president of Brazil told the United Nations that if the Western
economies don't get going again and devote part of their new wealth to
keeping Brazil in business, then the whole world will face a depression of

1930's magnitude. Keep lending, the president was telling the industrial West, otherwise we will go down and sure as hell pull you down with us!

M. de Larosière and his American monetary colleagues are saying much the same thing—just as ominously—for as we have already seen, they have told the large banks of the world that the IMF and its member governments will lend billions of dollars in the form of bailout funds to Brazil, but *only* if the commercial banks which are already up to their ears in loans to that country *increase* their net exposure by 7 percent a year! In other words, either you throw more good money after bad, or else you are on your own, fellows. So what choice does *your* banker have but to allocate still more of *your* savings for export? None, for the Federal Reserve Board of the United States has quietly passed the word that those "bankers who did not go along with such increases might find their Mexican loans coming under closer scrutiny by Federal Reserve bank examiners," according to the New York *Times*.

In other words, *either* they make *new* bad foreign loans, involving the export of more domestic savings, *or* the Fed might call some of their *old* bad foreign loans bad loans, which they are anyway. Thus, when they are accused of bailing out the banks, the people running the Fed and the IMF can quite justifiably claim, "We are not bailing them *out*, we are bailing them *in*."

As we shall see in the next chapter, pessimists feel that the banks are going to be bailed in well over their heads one of these years and the result will be a global credit collapse. Then, they say, only someone with gold bars stashed away will survive financially. When we discuss gold as an investment still further along in this book, we will consider the merits of this thesis and indicate whether prudence calls for the inclusion of at least *some* gold in your investment portfolio.

But what about route number two? What about funding the deficits through *domestic* borrowing *without* monetary expansion? This is what we tried as recently as 1981, when the new President, Reagan, and the Carter-appointed chairman of the Federal Reserve Board, Paul Volcker, had to finance a $100 billion deficit and decided that if they wanted to reverse the tide of inflation, the only way to do it was to fund the deficit through domestic borrowing *without* any accommodation from the central bank.

Result: Under pressure of federal borrowing, the prime interest rate went over 20 percent; three-month Treasury bills went to 17 percent; long-term Treasury bonds went to 14 percent; the economy collapsed into the longest and deepest recession since the 1930's; unemployment climbed to over 10 percent and stayed there for a long time.

To be sure, inflation *did* fall from Carter's 13 percent rate to 3 percent two years later under the Reagan/Volcker regime. But if Reagan and the Fed achieved this primary goal, the cost of that achievement was so painful that the people of the United States are unlikely to pay it again in this decade.

Yet we Americans will probably be faced with just such a choice much sooner than most of us think. For by the time this book is published we may be facing the next crossroads when we will have to decide between more inflation and yet another recession—the third in the string of recessions which have plagued our society since the beginning of 1980. If we are not lucky, we may end up with both. For what could happen next is this: in the pull of the current economic recovery, private sector demand for credit—which remained low during the 1981–82 recession—will come back strongly in 1984–85, as it always does in the second stage of *every* recovery. What will be *new* this time is that such private demand for credit will collide head-on with government borrowings which are twice as great as they have ever been before, government borrowings which are already absorbing close to 100 percent of all new net savings being produced by the American economy. lose faith in US ⇒ foreign investors will flee

If the Federal Reserve then stays "neutral"—leaving the credit markets to their own fate—and neither expands nor contracts the money and credit supply, then the possibility arises of a credit crunch to end all credit crunches and a return to 1981 in spades with killer interest rates, a diving economy and, this time around, since we would be starting from a much higher unemployment base left over from the last recession, unemployment rates in the 13–14 percent range or worse.

But as I have said, Americans will not accept this outcome. Reagan talked us into it once; he will not be able to talk us into it twice.

So *if* such a credit crunch were to develop in, say, 1985, and *if* the "Reagan option" is out, as I think it is, then what we have left is the "Johnson option." We can reflate the supply of money and credit, flooding the markets with enough liquidity so that high demand for credit from both the public and private sectors can be accommodated simultaneously, and hope that the recovery will last forever.

Such monetary expansion is the third and last of de Larosière's options for funding deficits. The results, for our personal investments could be disastrous, however, because under current global conditions de Laro-

(Tax bill → discourage saving ↓ many. less saving in the future)
growth -is needed to stop long run inflation

sière's third option would require "accommodation" by the Fed on a scale that is frightening even to contemplate. For the Fed will have to expand the money supply enough to allow IBM and Ford and TWA and farmers and new house buyers to borrow the vast sums they need while at the same time making sure that the banks have enough money to grant Mexico and Brazil and so on their annual 7 percent net loan increases, to allow Sweden and France and Denmark—not to speak of the IMF itself—to get their annual borrowing "fix," while at the same time providing the Treasury of the United States with more than $200 billion to cover its deficits. The overall objective of such explosive monetary expansion would be to provide so much liquidity that interest rates would remain steady, or even fall.

With net private savings in the United States today amounting to less than $200 billion—with net private *world* savings amounting to only $500 billion—the amount of funding that the Fed would have to provide to fill the gap between demand for credit and the supply of savings available would be unprecedented in our history.

The danger, of course, is that while such expansion might temporarily solve the liquidity problem, it would also accelerate the return of high rates of inflation, which would inevitably bring much higher rates of interest. The threat of a return of double-digit inflation and interest rates would be a disaster for all private investors holding bonds in their portfolios. But the massacre would not be restricted to fixed-interest securities. As the bond market collapsed, the probability is very high that the stock market would do the same. Thus *all* "financial" assets would once again be in trouble, just as they were in the second half of the 1970's when both inflation and interest rates got out of hand. As in the 1970's, "real" assets —precious metals, real estate, diamonds, oil and gas—would once again be the place for one's money.

The return of renewed financial chaos would no doubt stop economic growth dead in its tracks. We would be right back where we started from, or worse: at best we would see a return to stagflation; at worst we would find ourselves sliding into that "triple-dip" recession which could be the worst we've ever seen.

In my judgment this *could* happen. So let's now look at a possible scenario for the next four years based upon such a set of pessimistic hypotheses. Later we'll take a more optimistic view.

Chapter 9

o◯oo◯oo◯o

The Next Four Years:
A Pessimistic Forecast

Stage 1: As the current recovery approaches its peak, and as the slack in the economy is eliminated, inflation starts to rise sharply.

Stage 2: The Fed, belatedly, cuts back on the growth of money supply in order to retard prices before they get out of hand. However, heavy borrowings by the private sector are colliding in earnest with the immense borrowing needs of the government. This collision, accompanied by monetary restraint, results in a crowding-out of the private sector as *short-term* interest rates rise quickly.

Stage 3: Almost every politician in the country now fears a rerun of 1981–82, except worse, for this time the recession could really become a depression should the latent banking crisis turn real as the onset of a severe economic relapse pushes a whole host of vulnerable countries and corporations into outright default. The Fed then has no choice but to cave in and provide enough liquidity for everyone. The brief interlude of monetary restraint ends. As money supply is once again allowed to rise, *short-*term interest rates are temporarily stabilized, or might even fall. The Fed, in defending its actions, points to the fact that Switzerland, for instance, allowed its M1 to grow at an annual rate of 18 percent from 1977 through much of 1979, yet the Swiss consumer price index subsequently rose at a rate of only 1.6 percent.

Stage 4: As the so-called "market participants"—the insiders—see through this and realize what is *really* happening, inflationary expectations again rise sharply. *Long-*term interest rates soon follow.

Stage 5: With long-term borrowing prohibitive, borrowers from General Motors to the Treasury of the United States once more turn increasingly to short-term instruments to meet their credit needs.

Stage 6: Short-term rates now begin to rise rapidly, the economy begins to stagnate, and with every indicator moving the wrong way, confidence in the future collapses, and so does the economy.

The pessimistic scenario ends with a bloated money supply, a high rate of inflation, extremely high interest rates and zero or negative growth. Graphically, it would look like Figure 12.

FIGURE 12
The Possible Paths of Money Supply, Inflation, Interest Rates, and
Output in the United States: A Pessimistic Forecast

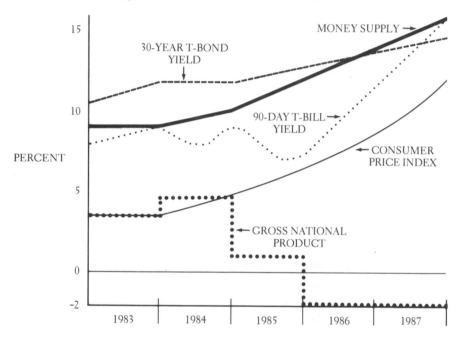

The four variables here—money supply, inflation, interest rates and output—would react upon one another to produce the ultimate disaster, a return to both recession and inflation. Let's track the chain reaction which, according to the pessimists, starts now with the current huge borrowing needs of governments here and abroad. These will soon collide with rising borrowing needs of the private sector. To "save" the recovery, monetary restraint will be abandoned. Renewed rapid creation of new money will follow. The ensuing inflation will lead to rising interest rates in 1985–86 and finally to a renewed collapse of confidence, and stagflation or deep recession. Let's look at these four variables in turn.

Money Supply and Inflation

I do a once-a-week radio call-in show called "Money Talk" in San Francisco: people call in and we talk about money. It is guaranteed that every other week somebody telephones to ask me to explain exactly how the government "prints" money. Everybody seems to know that when a government does that, what eventually results is inflation. Everybody also seems to understand that the process does not involve a huge printing press located somewhere in Washington grinding out greenbacks, but rather a highly complicated, almost mystical, process which, my callers strongly suspect, can only be understood by the Rockefellers, the Trilateral Commission and maybe the Russians, all of whom are out to control the world at our expense through their manipulation of the Federal Reserve system.

Rather than my going through a long technical description of the process, I hope you will be satisfied with this: All that happens is that the Federal Reserve creates new money when it buys securities from the Treasury. Since by law the Fed cannot buy them directly except in times of extreme national emergency, it does so by going through a complicated rigmarole involving open-market operations. What happens is that the Federal Reserve buys Treasury securities in the market and pays for them by crediting the reserve accounts of the sellers' banks. Because banks are required to maintain reserves equal to a percentage of their deposits, an increase in their reserves adds to the banks' ability to increase their deposits and to make additional loans and investments, thus adding to the money supply.

Next step: you have to accept on faith the fact that all money is not created equal. As un-American as this may sound, we have three classes of money, M_1, M_2 and M_3. M_1 is made up of cash and private checking accounts, and now amounts to an aggregate in excess of half a trillion dollars. M_2 is M_1 plus "saving money" plus Eurodollars. It adds up to a figure approaching \$2.3 trillion. When you add "institutional money," chiefly jumbo CDs (certificates of deposit in amounts of \$100,000 and greater), to M_2, you get M_3, which amounts to around \$2.7 trillion.

Money-supply watchers watch M_1 almost exclusively because it is the only money-supply aggregate that is reported weekly. Each Friday afternoon, after the securities markets in New York close, the Federal Reserve announces the amount of M1 in circulation, albeit not the amount out-standing *that* week but rather the M1 that *was* in circulation at the end of the *prior* week. M2 and M3 figures are given only once a month.

M1 is watched so closely not only because it can be tracked on a current basis but also because it is recognized as the "hot" money in our system, the money that all of us use for our daily and weekly transactions. M1—cash and our private checking accounts—is the "transactional" money that is constantly "chasing" groceries and gasoline and home computers. As we all know, if too much money chases too few goods, we usually get inflation.

But the pessimists don't say *usually,* they say we *always* get inflation when M1 grows at an excessive rate. The link between inflation and changes in M2 or M3 is much less direct, as studies done by the Federal Reserve Bank of St. Louis have consistently shown: thus the preoccupa-tion with M1. But what is excessive? It is usually defined as a rate of M1 growth higher than the increase in national output, or about 3–5 percent in our low-growth environment. How soon do we get inflation after money supply starts to grow too quickly? Inflation usually builds up after a lag of eighteen months to two years.

Look at the record (Figure 13). The 8.5 percent growth in M1 in 1972–73 produced 11 percent inflation in 1975. A return to that same 8.5 percent growth in M1 in 1978 produced well over 10 percent inflation in 1981.

Question: How fast did M1 grow in 1983? Answer: *at a rate that was higher than in both 1972–73 and 1978.*

What more is there to say? the pessimists ask. The inflationary writing is on the American wall and there is no escape. Paul Volcker has led us down the garden path. While seeking reappointment as chairman of the Fed in the summer of '83 he presented himself as the last of the inflation-fighters. Nobody wanted to notice that it was he who had been jacking up M1 at a rate without precedent in recent times: it grew at a 14 percent clip from July 1982 to May 1983.

Volcker's monetary chickens, bred in 1982–83, will *inevitably* come home to roost in 1985–86, the pessimists say. The result will be not 11 percent inflation but 15 percent. That's why long-term bond yields are 12 percent already, as Milton Friedman pointed out. However, when the Fed panics—really panics—in 1985–86, first by futilely trying to reverse course and then by letting M1 grow even faster then than it did in 1983, what will happen is that during the *next* two years that 15 percent rate of inflation could become 20 percent or more. This buildup in inflation will

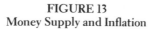

FIGURE 13
Money Supply and Inflation

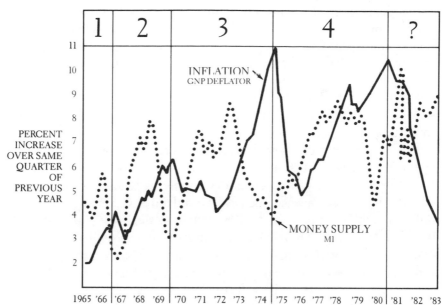

be reinforced by the fact that the velocity of money—the number of times in the course of a year that the money supply is spent and respent—increases as inflation rises. Who wants to leave cash lying around the house when it buys 2 percent less every month? So people learn to get rid of cash as fast as it comes in when prices are rising rapidly. With both money supply *and* velocity increasing, there will be a lot of hot money chasing the goods in our system and who knows where inflation might end up in 1988.

So only fools are not preparing to protect themselves now, the pessimists say. How does one do that? Well, first, how not. It was the great Paul Samuelson, the first American economist to win the Nobel Prize, who, it is reported, told the President's Council of Economic Advisers in the 1960's that anyone who did not protect himself from inflation by buying corporate equities was so stupid that he deserved to lose his wealth. So what happened? Between the mid-1960's and the early 1980's stocks *lost* well over half their value in terms of purchasing power. In August 1982, when it became apparent that the recession of 1981–82 had broken the back of inflation, the market finally turned upward. But with that brief respite from inflation expected to end by 1985, according to the pessimists, only very great fools indeed would follow Samuelson's advice a second time.

No, the place to be when double-digit inflation is just around the corner is not in financial assets, it's in *real* assets. So sell your stocks, dump your bonds, empty out your money market account and head for gold, silver, diamonds, real estate, oil and gas, the pessimists advise. That's where the smart people made their money between 1975 and 1980 when inflation was building up, and that's where the smart people are again going to make their money between 1985 and 1990 when the same inflationary spiral returns.

Where else lies protection? In the currencies of those countries which *consistently* regard inflation as the number one enemy in their society, countries where the control of money supply has traditionally taken on almost religious significance, such as Switzerland or Germany. It has been stated, probably correctly so, that *everybody* at the Swiss National Bank, the Swiss counterpart of our Fed, is a monetarist. So get ready to dump dollars and buy Swiss francs and marks. Everybody knows, the pessimists add, that the dollar is still wildly overvalued. First that overvaluation will be corrected. Then the dollar will continue its downward spiral losing all attraction to foreigners as a store of value, as inflation revives in the United States. They will dump the rest of their dollar holdings and the Swiss franc will go to 1.50; the mark to 1.75. As an American you'll clean up if you beat the foreigners to the draw and get into these currencies *now* before the run on the dollar starts in earnest.

Interest Rates and Output

As I already indicated, the pessimists' scenario does not call for all this to happen in a straight line. *Before* the inflationary floodgates are opened, the monetary authorities are going to attempt a last stand against the inevitable. They will slam on the monetary brakes. M1 growth will be reduced to near zero in an effort to shock inflationary expectations out of the system.

This zig-zag interlude will probably not come until 1985. But it will come. And it won't work. Monetary restraint should have been exercised at the *beginning* of the recovery in order to moderate economic growth and prevent too great a buildup in credit needs by the private sector. But Volcker, under pressure by the Reagan Administration, which wanted to go into the 1984 elections on the crest of an economic boom, did not do this. He let M1 grow at the torrid rate of 14 percent between the summer of 1982 and the summer of 1983. To be sure, during the second half of 1983 Volcker temporarily cut that growth rate to 3 percent. But it is widely felt that M1 growth will be back up in the 9+ percent range this year. For it is feared, and no doubt correctly so, that monetary restraint in 1984 could abort the recovery and endanger Reagan's reelection. Remember, though the Fed is independent, its chairman is a Republican and would hardly like to see the nation's monetary affairs taken over by an appointee of a newly elected Democrat in the White House.

So the barn door was left open; the opportunity to practice gradualism in monetary policy was missed. Thus after the monetary excesses of the 1982–84 period, the only remaining course of correction left to the Fed in 1985 will be to slam on the brakes, brutally. But to cut back the money supply then in an atmosphere of intense demand for funds from both the private and public sectors will, of course, send short-term interest rates sharply upwards.

When this happens, the pessimists say, you will have your last chance, dear investor, to save your wealth by moving it into *real* assets. If the pessimists are right, it would pay you to take a closer look at this interlude of severe monetary restraint which, they say, will immediately precede the opening of the monetary floodgates after mid-decade.

How will you spot this moment? After all, such decisions affecting money-supply growth are made in secret by the Open Market Committee of the Fed and not made public until two months later—when it is too late for you and me to protect ourselves.

Watch two indicators: the federal funds interest rate and the rate being offered by banks in London for thirty-day and ninety-day Eurodollar deposits. Though the Fed tightens money and credit in secret, banks notice the effect within a couple of days as market liquidity dries up. The banks that were least liquid to begin with immediately start to scramble around for funds, "buying" money where it is still available. The first place they go is to other banks that still have excess reserves with the Fed. The price they pay for the overnight borrowing of such funds from other banks is published the next day in your newspaper as the federal funds rate. When that rate suddenly goes up sharply and keeps going up, you will know that the credit crunch is probably beginning. The confirmation of this will come from the thirty- and ninety-day Eurodollar rates. When banks start to bid those rates up, they are not just committing themselves overnight, as in the case of fed funds, but for a longer period. That means that they believe that what's happening is not just a market quirk, but the result of a deliberate action by the Federal Reserve. So they seek to protect themselves by buying longer-term dollars in large amounts in London while they are still "cheap."

Most daily newspapers around the country have a "box" in the fine print at the end of the business section which gives a complete run-down of prevailing interest rates. A sample is shown in Figure 14. If and when it looks as if the "pessimistic" scenario is about to phase in, it would pay you to look up, and then track, these key interest rates on a regular basis.

FIGURE 14
Interest Rates

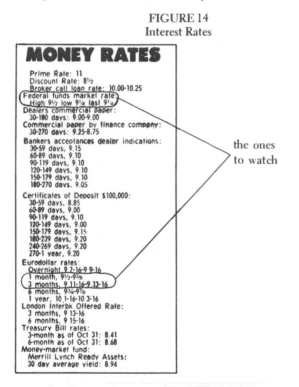

These initial interest rate increases will represent the last warning bell telling you to get out of financial assets. This does not just mean the bond market, the pessimists warn. Such interest rate changes will represent the precursors of the end of the bull stock market as well. The market took off in the summer of 1982, they remind us, because interest rates finally started to move down decisively. That established the market *trend*. Along that trend, short-term moves in the bull market continued to be affected almost exclusively by short-term interest rates. When the prime rate went down a point, the market went up 50–75 points; another point down in interest rates, another 50 points up in the Dow. When interest rates occasionally got stuck for a while, so did the market. Well, what was true on the up-side is going to be equally true on the down-side. As the prime goes back to 12 percent, then 13 percent, the market will start to ratchet down 50 points at a time. As inflation rates soar, a down trend will be confirmed and we will have entered the bear market of 1985–86. Joe Granville will be back in style.

What happens next is that as interest rates rise, big trouble looms for the output of the economy. Housing and automobiles—the prime engines of growth in the American economy—cannot prosper when interest rates become prohibitive and scare off buyers. The ripples sent out result in sharply falling demand for everything from lumber to tires to glass. The United States will find itself in the *third* recession of the decade and the 1980's will be barely half over! The stock market, which by now will be down hundreds of points, will, again, have proven to be an excellent "predictor" of where the economy is headed.

At this point the international debt situation will kick in. Because interest rates on Third World loans are directly indexed to the Eurodollar rate, every 1 percent rise in dollar interest rates increases the cost of Third World debt service by $5 billion a year; 3 points, $15 billion.

How will the debtor nations bear this additional burden? They have no choice but to borrow yet more despite the fact that the debt situation has already escalated to the point where Mexico faces total interest and debt repayments of $38 billion in 1987. The banks, in turn, have no choice but to lend this additional $15 billion, maybe by now $20 billion, to the LDCs to keep them afloat.

So despite the fact that money is now a scarce commodity in New York and London and everywhere else as a result of the credit crunch initiated by the Fed, the commercial banks up north are now going to have to raise that $15–$20 billion in addition to the money they must come up with to provide these same Third World debtors with their annual 7 percent fix. How will the banks attract the needed funds? By ratcheting up interest rates still further. The long-term outlook now turns bleak. As killer interest rates force the United States, and then the entire industrialized West, into yet another recession, hope for that ultimate "solution" of the debt dilemma—sustained economic growth—will fade, maybe once and for all.

And what will happen to Citibank or Chase? Under these circumstances, would *you* want to keep uninsured funds with a bank that has lent twice its net worth out there?

Not us, say the pessimists.

The hard-core pessimists claim that there is a real danger that *if* the monetary authorities take this tack, and *if* they stay the monetary restraint course too long, then the game will be over right there and then. The international banking system will collapse and the world economy will collapse along with it. Therefore, they say, it will *not* happen this way.

Instead, precisely *because* this ultimate crisis *must* be avoided, the Fed will have no choice but to do another monumental flip-flop and once again flood the financial markets with liquidity. The interlude of brutal monetary restraint will have been a brief one. M1 growth will now accelerate from zero to an annual rate of 15 percent or higher, as it did in 1982. The *acute* crisis will be avoided. Interest rates will stop rising, probably even retreat temporarily. But not for long. Because although additional liquidity will temporarily check the explosion of short-term rates and will allow the recovery to continue, as the Fed continues to push money into the markets inflationary expectations will soar, and so will *long-*term interest rates. There we have it; the pessimists' viewpoint in a nutshell:

> If the Federal Reserve *does* "support" the financing of both future U.S. deficits and the borrowings of foreign governments in the dollar area *and* the financing of a recovering private sector, higher interest rates will result.
>
> *Cause:* inflationary expectations.
>
> If the Federal Reserve *does not* "support" the financing of such governmental deficits and borrowings, higher interest rates will result.
>
> *Cause:* crowding out and a banking crisis.

Hobson's choice. In both cases higher interest rates are inevitable. And as interest rates rise, the economies of the world will sink.

Final result: the recession will merely have been postponed. By 1987 it will hit the United States with full, brutal force. Maybe sooner.

As business activity decreases and unemployment increases—this time heading for 13 percent or even 14 percent of the labor force—tax receipts will immediately start to fall off as unemployment-related government expenditures rise sharply. For every 1 percent increase in unemployment the deficit will grow by $30 billion. By 1987 the deficit will be approaching $300 billion, or 8 percent of GNP. With net private savings at 7 percent of GNP, this will mean that 125 percent of net savings in the United States are now being absorbed by the government. Capital accumulation by the private sector is now virtually impossible. Productivity *has* to sink once more, and sink rapidly, as must real income.

As this malaise spreads to Western Europe, unemployment there will rise to 25 million, perhaps even 30 million. European deficits will now match those in the United States. European central banks will have to absorb billions of dollars fleeing the United States, convert them into marks and francs and guilders, causing their money supplies to soar, with the inevitable inflationary consequences. The alternative to this would be to see the international value of their currencies soar, making exporting yet more difficult, contributing to still higher unemployment.

As demand for Third World exports plummets throughout the industrialized world as a result of this now global inflationary recession, sovereign loan defaults on a massive scale are only a matter of time. There is now no way that Mexico can pay even half of that $38 billion which is coming due in 1987.

The Dow falls back to 750. Gold rises to $1200. Bond markets, worldwide, are dead. Not a pretty picture, you are perhaps saying. And perhaps you are also muttering, "Who needs a book like this, anyway?"

Well, don't give up yet because *maybe* things will turn out a whole lot better than the pessimists think. The "swing" factor, the variable which could drastically change the whole picture, is the potential rate of economic growth in the years immediately ahead. The Reagan Administration's budgetary forecasts are based upon an average growth of GNP of 4 percent through 1988. The pessimistic analysis assumes that this is too high—that because of the "drag" of continuing high interest rates we will be lucky to average 2 percent, and that the benchmark by which to judge these figures is the average rate of real economic growth in the United States during the past thirty years, which has been 3 percent.

However, maybe, just maybe, all three of these figures are too low. Should the United States shift onto a high growth plane, the result would be appreciably lower unemployment, substantially higher tax receipts, a drastic reduction in the deficit, which would radically reduce the need for enlarging the money supply, thus lowering inflationary expectations, in the wake of which both nominal as well as real interest rates would be much lower than anticipated.

Let's examine the feasibility of such a future.

Chapter 10

o◯oo◯oo◯o

The Next Four Years:
An Optimistic Forecast

B ACK A WAY, I suggested that perhaps growth was dead, at least for a while, because the preconditions for the type of sustained economic growth we enjoyed in the past no longer exist. I further suggested that in their absence, we were very vulnerable to external "shocks" which, when they hit, could repeatedly send us into extended periods of economic paralysis. Such preconditions were:

· low energy costs
· sustained low rates of inflation
· sustained low rates of interest, especially *real* interest
· rapidly expanding world trade
· a viable, integrated global banking system

But have these preconditions really disappeared? Perhaps I was wrong to suggest that they had. Maybe I was suffering from the illness that typically afflicts economists, the extrapolation disease—I mean the habit of taking current trends and projecting them *ad infinitum*.

Most suspect of all the items on this list is obviously the first one—that the days of cheap energy are lost and gone forever. But are they? Look at what has happened all of a sudden to the oil price. Instead of going from $40 a barrel to $60 to $100, it has dramatically reversed its course. From this *The Economist* drew the following conclusion:

There is hope that big industrialized countries may soon be flooded with cheaper and more abundant Middle East oil. This would provide an opportunity for a swing back out of the inflationary slump of 1973–83 into a falling-inflation boom of 1983–93. Cheap oil could be as reinvigorating to tired western economies as spinach was to Popeye.

Let's examine this thesis, and in the process reexamine those other preconditions for growth. Could the positive effects of a downward shift in oil prices also positively affect the outlook for inflation, interest rates, the banking system and even the trend toward protectionism to such a degree that OPEC's retreat has signaled the turning point, as *The Economist* suggests, from ten years of stagflation to a decade of prosperity?

Everything depends, of course, on how far the price of oil goes down and how long it stays down.

Let's look at the first two oil shocks. On October 5, 1973, the price of a barrel of oil from the Persian Gulf was $3.65. After the embargo precipitated by the Arab-Israeli conflict which started on October 6 of that year, the price *quintupled* to $17 a barrel. This was oil shock number one, and we've already seen its disastrous consequences for the West.

Shock number two came with the ascendancy of Khomeini in Iran, and the end of oil exports from that country. During the market squeeze that resulted, the posted price of crude oil in Saudi Arabia, which is the benchmark for all oil prices, went to $34 a barrel. In other words, the price of oil doubled. That was sufficient to trigger a few more years of stagflation in the West.

As everyone knows, the price of oil permeates every other aspect of economic activity. The only parallel is interest rates. Double interest costs and you create havoc throughout an economy . . . as we have seen. Halve them and you get economic recovery.

Halving oil prices would mean around $20–$22 a barrel if you look at the price in "real" terms (i.e., after adjusting for the inflation that has occurred during the past three years). Would that turn things around? I think the answer is obviously yes, depending on whether or not these new prices hold for a significant period of time. As with interest, lower rates really help only if "inflationary expectations" are such that everybody expects low rates to stay for a while—if they can plan on their doing so, then they make the rest of their plans accordingly.

So what are sound "oil cost expectations" today?

The answer will depend on how effective a cartel OPEC continues to be in the 1980's. That OPEC is substantially less effective than in the 1970's is already beyond doubt. At the end of that decade, world oil consumption was 50 million barrels a day; OPEC provided 31 million barrels of that, or over 60 percent. Today consumption has fallen to 45 million barrels a day, and of that, OPEC today provides less than 20 million barrels, or less than 40 percent.

The key to the survival of any supply cartel like OPEC is its power to establish and maintain a *dominant* market share, for only then can it set the price. De Beers, which controls the diamond market, provided the best example in modern times of how such a cartel functions. As long as De Beers controlled 85–90 percent of the total supply of new gems that were allowed to reach the world market, it could dictate the price. It did, and thus was able to "make" the price of diamonds go steadily and consistently up not just for a decade but over an entire generation. Ultimately De Beers was defeated by its own success, or perhaps a better word would be avarice. For once the price of diamonds went high enough, $60,000 a carat for the benchmark white ("D") flawless, new sources sprang into being—and an increasingly large uncontrolled flow of diamonds started to hit the market from places like Zaire and the Soviet Union and even from dealers—former "insiders" who, now attracted by once-in-a-lifetime prices, started going for the quick buck by dumping their inventories, bypassing De Beers. The price of that "D" flawless collapsed back down to $14,000 a carat within two years.

Bunker Hunt found out exactly the same thing. He thought that if he dominated the world's silver exchanges, he could make billions on that metal. He did, for a while at least. He drove the price from $3 an ounce to $45 an ounce. Evoked by that outrageous price, silver seemed to appear from everywhere—from India, from coinage, from new mines all over the place, from fellow speculators who were now bailing out, taking their profits. For a while Hunt tried to absorb it all, and in the process lost not only the billion he had made on the way up, but another one on the way down when his attempt to prevent a price collapse proved futile. Ultimately silver went back to $4.95 an ounce in mid-1982. Bunker went back to Texas.

Both of these cases are pertinent to the current oil situation. Sheik Ahmed Zaki Yamani has been to oil what Bunker was to silver: the man who thought he could control the price of his commodity through thick and thin simply because he, or at least the nation he represented, was richer than everybody else. Thus the Saudis concluded that they and the rest of the world could live comfortably with oil at $34 a barrel for quite a while. When in 1979 a continuing scarcity of crude threatened to result in another major price upswing, Saudi Arabia dramatically increased its output from the 8 million barrels a day it normally sustained to 11.5 million barrels. The threatened scarcity disappeared and world prices again settled in at around $34 a barrel, the Saudi benchmark. But that $34-a-barrel price has, in retrospect, been to oil what $45 an ounce was to silver and what $60,000 a carat was to diamonds: it greatly discouraged demand and greatly encouraged the development of new supply. Predictably, two things happened: world consumption dropped sharply, the result of worldwide energy conservation; and worldwide recession occurred, both provoked by oil at $34 a barrel. Just as high silver prices had brought silver out of India, and high diamond prices brought gems out of Zaire, so also non-OPEC output—in Mexico, in the North Sea, in Canada, in the Soviet Union—began to soar and an oil glut began to build.

The Saudis reacted consistently. They cut their output drastically from 11.5 million barrels a day all the way back to 3 million barrels and insisted that every other producing country within OPEC practice similar output restraint and help defend that $34 price. Some did, some didn't. But the chief sinner within the cartel was Saudi Arabia's archenemy, Iran.

Iranian output, which one had thought would remain insignificant for years due to both domestic chaos and the ongoing war with Iraq, suddenly rebounded from zero in 1979 to 2.5 million barrels a day by 1983, and seemed destined to keep rising back up toward the 5–6 million-barrel-a-day range where it was during the last shah's heyday. The problem Iran's rising output created for OPEC was compounded by the fact that an increasing percentage of Iranian crude was now being sold on the Rotterdam spot market at prices below the cartel price—$30 a barrel, then $29, then $28.

When Yamani then called an OPEC meeting in London, everybody came. He agreed to a new benchmark price for Saudi crude of $29 a barrel, and OPEC agreed to a ceiling of 17.5 million barrels a day. Yet less than a month later Iran was already making deals with one of Saudi Arabia's largest traditional customers, Japan, at prices below the agreed minimum.

With OPEC's market position broken as a result of rising output from elsewhere—with additional oil soon to be gushing from new wells in Africa, Latin America and even China in the near future and with hopes of maintaining internal discipline a mirage—with Iran and Iraq at each other's throats on the battlefield, with Saudi Arabia backing Iraq to prevent Iranian hegemony of the Persian Gulf, with Gaddafi out to scuttle everybody, with Nigeria and Venezuela desperate for income to service their immense external debts—there is little doubt that the world is going to enjoy at least a couple of years of much lower oil costs.

But it would be folly to believe that this respite is going to last much longer than that. Though it would be a mistake to overwork the parallels, remember that after the price of silver collapsed—all the way back to $4.95 in early 1982—a year later it bounced back up above $14 an ounce. Nor did the collapse of diamond prices and the demise of De Beers, forecast by Edward Jay Epstein in his book *The Rise and Fall of Diamonds: The Shattering of a Brilliant Illusion,* occur. Zaire returned to the fold, and so did the Soviet Union. Even the much-feared new producer of diamonds, Australia, joined the cartel. That benchmark diamond price which bottomed at $14,000 has been rising ever since.

Nevertheless, as I write, lower oil prices are here and are going to stay with us for quite a while. The computer of the OECD (the Organization for Economic Cooperation and Development, the Paris-based organization that embraces all of Western Europe, North America and Japan— i.e., the industrialized West) figures that each 10 percent drop in the oil price will

1. Increase the *entire area's* growth by 0.5 percent per annum.
2. Cut back the rate of inflation throughout the area by 1 percent per annum.

An oil price in the $20 to $24 range would represent a 30 to 40 percent drop, producing up to a 1.5–2 percent rise in growth and a 3 percent fall in the rate of inflation.

Early in 1983 both the *Wall Street Journal* and *Forbes* magazine gave prominent space to the prediction of a certain Alan Reynolds of Polyeconomics, Inc., one of the nation's many economic forecasting groups. He said that all the talk about quarter-trillion-dollar deficits, and the potential disastrous consequences they will have for our economic future, is nonsense, the result of faulty estimating procedures by government. Reynolds claims that "raising real growth by a half percentage point above an average recovery could conceivably balance the budget by 1985."

Well, let's figure it out. The rate of real growth that prevails during the "average recovery" has been 4 percent historically, and this is the rate used by the Reagan Administration for budgeting purposes. Bump that up to 4.5, according to our man from Polyeconomics, and we are already out of the woods. But our friend the OECD computer says that at $24 a barrel we can bump growth up by one to two full percentage points. That would mean 5–6 percent growth! Wow!

The logic behind this is sound, thanks to the tremendous "leverage" inherent in fiscal policy. Bump growth up just a bit, in percentage terms, and two exaggerated responses follow. At higher income levels, and even with the same tax rates, tax receipts swell as more people go back to work and rejoin the tax rolls. On the expenditure side, "exaggerated" benefits also accrue rapidly as the cost of everything from unemployment insurance benefits to food stamps drops off precipitously while unemployment plummets and the economy grows. Thus every 1 percent drop in unemployment in the United States reduces the deficit by $25 to $30 billion. Go back to 7 percent unemployment, which a 5–6 percent annual growth rate would probably produce, and that would mean *annual* improvements of $75 billion to $90 billion.

This would probably not result in a balanced budget for 1985, but sustained real growth at the 5–6 percent level would surely result in future deficits half the size currently projected. This would mean that as private-sector borrowing began to pick up—raising the specter of a giant credit crunch—public-sector borrowing would begin to plummet, eliminating that specter before it even materialized. With income rising, gross savings available to the nation's capital markets would rise sharply even if savings rates themselves did not increase. Thus, looking at it strictly from the flow-of-funds point of view, you could have a very strong recovery, followed by a very strong revival in private-sector borrowing offset in the capital markets by a marked drop in competitive borrowing from the government and a high level of inflow of new funds from higher savings.

This would solve the crowding-out problem. Nominal interest rates would stay in the single-digit range indefinitely, and if inflation remained low, real interest rates would then return to "normal."

Consider another optimistic voice, that of Evan Galbraith, now U.S. ambassador to France and before that one of the world's more innovative investment bankers. He thinks that there won't be a crowding-out in any case. Like Reynolds, he feels that the pessimists are using faulty estimating procedures. What he says, correctly I think, is that "most discussions of the [potential] crowding out of private borrowers focus on a comparison between annual *net* private savings in the U.S. and projected budget deficits. These comparisons show U.S. budget deficits approaching the level of net private savings."

The result, Galbraith correctly concludes, would be that federal borrowing would crowd private borrowers out and would force medium- and long-term rates up inordinately, thwarting economic recovery. But, he then says, "this comparison is based on an important miscalculation."

The figure we must look at, Galbraith says, is not *net* private savings but *gross* private savings. The difference is depreciation. Gross includes it, net subtracts it. What Galbraith says is that the cash represented by depreciation is left with the private owners, corporate or individual, who use it mostly for self-financing. Because self-financing takes the pressure off the market, it is as important as cash that goes directly to the market.

If he is right, it would sure make a difference, to put it mildly. While net private savings in 1982, for example, were $189 billion, if you add depreciation (or capital consumption allowances) of $360 billion, then you get gross private savings of $549 billion. Against this figure, total government borrowing needs of $200 billion will hardly crowd out the private sector. In fact even with *total* borrowing in the $500 billion range, as it is now, there would be no crowding-out. (What Galbraith forgets is that if you add the "invisible" nonmarket funds available from depreciation to one side of the equation, you must also add the "invisible" projects that they finance to the grand figures representing the "borrowing" needs necessary to finance such projects to the other side, with the result that you end up with the same net figure.)

Galbraith concludes that his theory explains "why we haven't seen the effect of crowding out. The market absorbed large private and federal financing in 1982, but interest rates fell." But Galbraith is wrong here too. The reason that the market could accommodate both public and private borrowings with falling interest rates in 1982 was that the United States was in its deepest recession since the 1930's. With the economy operating at 67 percent of capacity, very few businesses in the United States were willing to borrow except to consolidate short-term debt. The rise in government borrowing was more than compensated for by the fall in private-sector borrowing. The test of the capital markets, whether you use gross or net savings, is going to come when the recovery is well under way and when private borrowers return to the market in quantity. Then, for the first time in history, they will be competing with government borrowing needs in twelve, *yes, twelve, digits.* Then we shall see the *first* true test of our capital markets in the 1980's.

Hugo Uyterhoeven, who teaches at the Harvard Business School, approaches the subject from yet another angle and has a better theory than Galbraith's. He says that the combination of recovery and very modest inflation through 1984 *is going to provide a foundation for four more years of boom thereafter.* The key, he says, is labor costs. The 1981–82 recession so chastened labor that we can expect annual compensation increases in the 6 percent range in the immediate future, combined with productivity increases in the 3 percent range, meaning that unit labor costs will only rise at 3 percent per annum, which, under the cost-push theory of inflation (where companies, when faced with increases in wages, increase their prices by approximately the same amount in order to protect their profit margins), will produce a rate of inflation in the same range. This would be in contrast to, say, 1980, when 10 percent compensation gains were offset by zero percent increase in productivity, producing that 10 percent inflation that almost sank us all.

The question is whether the 1982 figures represent only a temporary effect of that year's recession or whether the inflationary wage-price spiral has *really* been broken. Uyterhoeven suggests the latter. And explains why by looking at the three variables involved, namely productivity, compensation and pricing.

Regarding productivity, he points out that during this past recession, business got significantly leaner and more efficient, with the result that productivity actually began rising during the recession proper, a very unusual phenomenon. With the onset of economic recovery in 1983, productivity began rising at an even faster rate. He suggests that this is because *attitudes* finally seem to have changed. No doubt this is so, but the rise in productivity was primarily due to the fact that unemployment rose to almost 11 percent, meaning that the remaining smaller work force, if it wanted to stay working, had to put out more than it had been accustomed to during boom times. He further suggests, and I agree, that because of the immense excess physical capacity which has been left over from that recession, it will take at least two years of growth before productivity-inhibiting bottlenecks reappear. So he sees productivity gains of 3 to 4 percent during the current recovery stage.

There are those who would disagree and suggest that *overall* "slack" does very little to eliminate bottlenecks, since they tend to crop up in exactly those places that are so "odd" that their sudden appearance cannot be anticipated. However, after a recession, inventories tend to be much larger than "normal," meaning that replacement parts or supplies are generally readily available, enabling producers to bridge a "crisis" until the bottleneck in the production process itself is eliminated. At the peak of booms with inventories depleted, this is not possible. So Uyterhoeven remains right on the productivity outlook, even though he has failed to provide the full explanation for it.

Meanwhile he sees wage increases now "locked in" for the next couple of years in the 5–7 percent range as a result of labor's bitter experience of the recent past with unemployment. Match that with 4 percent productivity gains and you get 3–4 percent *real* pay increases. This would stand in stark contrast to the years since 1978, during which inflation consistently exceeded nominal wage increases, resulting in a decline in the purchasing power of the average paycheck and in the standard of living of a large percentage of the American population. This turnaround will encourage further moderation in nominal wage claims as the decade progresses. Skeptics would doubt this and claim that labor will get what it can, when and where the opportunity arises: that vengeance, not contrition, will rule. I tend to agree with the skeptics.

As for pricing, the question is whether businesses will now try to recoup recession losses by jacking up prices as prosperity returns. They won't, Uyterhoeven claims, because if they do, the damn Democrats will regain the White House. Here he is obviously overplaying his hand: no businessman has *ever* forgone a price increase for *this* reason, not even one of Ronnie Reagan's pals in southern California. But, Uyterhoeven continues, they won't *have* to raise prices anyway: tax cuts, lower energy costs and lower overheads resulting from fixed-cost paring during the recession will leave them with ample future profit margins.

Regarding interest costs, our man from Harvard Business School also has a theory. He says this: Real rates of interest of 7 percent (the difference between the nominal rates of interest and inflation) are "ridiculously high," echoing the words of Helmut Schmidt when he was still West Germany's chancellor, who said that real interest rates were at the highest level in the 2,000 years since Jesus Christ. While high real interest rates can be justified as a potential inflation hedge—a nominal 12 percent interest rate now merely anticipates a 10 percent rate of inflation later—the need for such a hedge disappears once enough people become convinced that inflation has indeed been brought under control. When that happens, the supply of money, which is after all only another commodity, will respond to price, i.e., still-too-high nominal rates will suck money out of the woodwork just as the $45-an-ounce price sucked out silver, or the $34-a-barrel price did oil. Result: a *money* glut! Cheap money means an explosive, extensive recovery as we all rush out to make those purchases which we have been postponing for years.

Rich at last!

So at least some of the "preconditions" for growth may actually be at hand:

· *Low energy costs:* The oil glut and the resulting disarray of OPEC are giving us, if not "low" energy costs, at least energy costs that are a lot lower than we had thought possible in the 1980's.

· *Sustained low rates of inflation:* The 1981–82 recession knocked inflation back to 3 percent, and if Professor Uyterhoeven is right about the future path of productivity relative to wage demands, it will stay there.

· *Sustained low rates of interest, especially real interest:* If both Professor Uyterhoeven and Ambassador Galbraith are right, we will not only have no global credit crunch in our future (since we have ample savings to feed the credit markets) but in fact we may end up with a money glut, meaning single-digit nominal interest rates indefinitely, and real interest rates back down where they belong—near zero.

Regarding the fourth precondition for renewed prosperity, the need for *rapidly expanding world trade,* I guess it could be argued that the current trend toward protectionism and global trade stagnation will be reversed should we embark upon five years of 3 percent inflation and 4 percent growth. Demand for raw materials in the industrialized world would reach new heights, reviving exports from the Third World. Furthermore, as unemployment receded throughout the West, the anti-Japanese forces for protectionism would ebb as well, allowing trade in manufactured goods to grow again.

This leads us to the fifth condition for economic revival, *a viable, integrated global banking system.* It has already been suggested that the ultimate solution to the financial bind that the banks find themselves in, relative to those forty-odd countries which today hover on the edge of default, is a recovery of the markets in the industrialized world. Higher demand for everything from cocoa to sugar to bauxite to bananas will eventually provide the Third World countries with sufficient income to start servicing their external debts in a normal fashion.

Paradoxically, it is the revival of growth that would restore these latter two preconditions for further growth, a sound banking system and expanded world trade. Which leaves us with a very big unanswered question. Where is all that growth supposed to come from? One can hardly look for sustained overall economic growth from steel, nor automobiles, nor tires, nor shoes, nor shipbuilding, nor textiles. These are all industries that are finished as the providers of growth, the principal creators of wealth, for Western society.

To be sure, if the price of oil went down to $8 a barrel (as Milton Friedman is suggesting it *should*), then gas would again cost fifty cents a gallon in the United States. Detroit could go back to building the only type of cars it builds well, gas-guzzling luxury liners, and the American public could again start buying the only type of cars it *really* loves, namely gas-guzzling luxury liners. Soon all of Michigan would be back at work, and as the automotive industry's demand for steel and glass and tires revived, so would the fortunes of the entire upper Midwest of the United States.

Unfortunately, that is not going to happen. The sun is setting *permanently* on America's smokestack industries. The combination of antiquated, inefficient plant and equipment, and labor costs double or triple those in places like South Korea or Brazil, simply means that we can no longer compete in world markets. Worse, we cannot even compete with foreign-made products of the smokestack-industry type in our *domestic* market. Global transportation costs in the 1980's are so low that they no longer "protect" the North American market from producers in Europe, Asia or Latin America, even where heavy, bulk items such as steel and cement are concerned.

So what have we left? What are the "sunrise" industries that are going to produce tomorrow's growth? We already know the answer: those involved in high technology. That narrows it down significantly, for it means predominantly electronics as applied to the fields of data-processing, instrumentation, communications, aerospace and defense systems.

The American electronics industry is the *global* well-spring for future sustained high-tech growth. American society encourages innovative entrepreneurship like none other. It allows, in fact it *encourages*, scientists/engineers/designers to break away from companies like IBM and Fairchild Semiconductor, to take their ideas with them and set up on their own. Try *that* in Germany, or in France, or in Switzerland, or, where it is *totally* impossible, in Japan. At best the industry would blackball you for the rest of your life; at worst you would go to jail for industrial espionage. Where I live in California they not only do neither, but people almost throw money at you in order to finance the development of your idea, hoping to get a "piece of the action" in the process. Venture capital is what we call it, and it is another area where the United States seems to have a truly unique position in the world.

The other industry where America has also taken a quantum leap forward relative to the rest of the world is genetic engineering. The initial applications have been in medicine. But a wide spectrum of applications for these techniques is apparent also in veterinary medicine, in agriculture and in energy transformation. New techniques promise a cure for foot-and-mouth disease, a plant that will grow potatoes below ground and tomatoes above, and processes to speed up metabolism to such a degree that "oil" can be created out of wood.

But though America leads today in these gene-splicing developments, tomorrow it will be challenged by Europe just as surely as Japan is already challenging our leadership in electronics. The transformation of society through the application of high technology is inevitably going to be a global process.

So the answer to the debt and deficit problems is growth, and the answer to the growth problem is the development of the high-technology industries which, as they come along, will send out ripple effects to revive "support" industries, ranging from housing to, yes, even automobiles. But such an acceleration of growth will by no means be restricted to ripple effects. It will be reinforced by the *internal* effects of the application of electronics to the work processes of *all* industries, sunrise and sunset. A study by the management consultancy firm of Booz Allen & Hamilton— one of the best in the field—indicates that the introduction of *already existing* office automation equipment, such as word processors, would boost office efficiency in the United States by 15 percent. This would mean a productivity gain of $300 billion *annually* for this country. The remaining question is: will it happen soon enough?

The optimists say yes. And since the United States still is to the rest of the world what we were once told General Motors was to the United States, such optimists claim that if we shift into high growth, the rest of the world will follow. Figure 15 summarizes the alternative path that may lie ahead of us—the high road into the future, which stands in stark contrast to the "low road" described in the previous chapter.

What would be the investment consequences of such a future? Obviously, the optimists claim, "financial assets" would remain king indefinitely. The Dow would move to 1,500, then 2,000, then 3,000 in an investment climate of sustained growth and steadily falling rates of inflation and interest. The bond rally of 1982 would be followed by the rally of '85 and the next of '87 as long-term interest rates went from 12 percent to 9 percent to 7 percent. On the other hand, you could forget about *ever* switching your money from stocks and bonds into "real" assets. With inflation dead, gold would end up at $250 an ounce, silver at $6, and no sane person would try to make money speculating in real estate during the rest of this decade. The dollar would reign as supreme in the 1980's as it had in the 1950's, so forget—permanently—about Swiss francs or yen as a hedge. There will be nothing to hedge against!

FIGURE 15
The Possible Paths of Money Supply, Inflation, Interest Rates, and
Output in the United States: An Optimistic Forecast

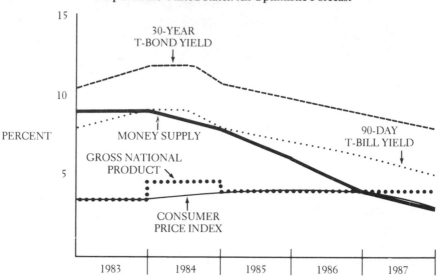

Thus should this low-inflation, high-growth scenario prove to be the right one for the next three years and beyond, obviously our private investment decisions would stand in stark contrast to those we would be making if we accept the "pessimistic" forecast. Or would they?

One by one we shall now examine each major type of investment available to us—from money market accounts and funds to gold to municipal bonds to stocks to real estate—and try to find the answer.

Part III

Investing
for the Future

Chapter 11

o◯oo◯oo◯o

Investing
for the Future

I BELIEVE THAT the key to *investing* for the future is to identify, well
ahead of time, where the *economy* is heading. It is especially important
to make sound judgments concerning the four key variables in our system
—money supply, inflation, interest rates and output. In this section I will
give you my *own* distinct views on the future path of these variables and
thus on the future of our economy, and my conclusions as to where you
should be investing *now,* and where you should be planning on investing
later.

I must stress that in this part of the book, I will be dealing mainly with
the next two years. As you will see, I view this short-run future with mild
optimism. Remember this, since the *investment* advice I give will be
colored by my belief that all those *economic* chickens out there are not
going to come home to roost in 1984, and maybe not even in 1985. I feel
that we are going to be blessed with a further period of grace.

But when I look *beyond* mid-decade, I worry, in fact at times I worry
a lot. I strongly suspect that the 1986 edition of this book will contain
investment suggestions that will be much more guarded, much more
defensive. For by then those storm clouds which are already evident on
the horizon today—debts, deficits, excessive growth in the money supply
and all the problems they bring—could well be gathering directly over-
head, and it will be time to run for cover.

Now I would like to make one suggestion before we examine the next
eighteen to twenty-four months in an investment context. While I think
we can all learn to track the economy and thus make good, logical basic
decisions on the *type* of investment we want at a given time, very few of

us have time to pick and choose carefully among the myriad possibilities that conform to this type, much less to monitor individual investments on a daily, weekly or monthly basis. Thus I would *strongly* advise against the do-it-all-yourself approach to personal investment.

The chances that an amateur will be able to beat the professionals in an ever-more-complicated investment world are slimmer every year. Why even try? We are fortunate to have a vast array of truly expert investment managers at our disposal in the United States. Use them! Don't always listen to them; in fact, make them listen to *you*. But *use* them. If you decide to get into the stock market, do it via a fund that has a management with a proven track record. Let that management then pick the stocks and make the switches and collect the dividends. When you decide to get out—because you sense that rising inflation is going to kill the *whole* market—don't *ask* their advice. Just *tell* them your decision. Then keep your money parked for a while in a money market account while you replot the future course of the economy in preparation for your next *fundamental* investment decision.

You, I am sure, do not believe that there are any magic formulas for making money. Neither do I. All I suggest is that you use your brains, do your homework, and then when you have figured out where our economy is going next, and thus where you want to invest next, go out and hire the best help you can.

Chapter 12

o◯ooᏫooᏫo

Money Market Funds
and Accounts

No MATTER WHICH PATH the economy follows this year, or for that matter for the next three or four years, one type of investment vehicle is going to provide a sure thing: the new money market accounts which are today available at most banks and savings and loans.

For these accounts now provide protection against *both inflation and default,* something that has heretofore not been available in our lifetime or probably anybody else's. This truly revolutionary advance came with the abolition of Regulation Q, the regulation under which the government established, by law, the upper limit on the interest rates that financial institutions could offer. For years and years it was 5.25 percent for banks and 5.5 percent for savings and loans, a rate that held regardless of the prevailing rate of inflation.

Regulation Q allowed the banks to—I'll try to find polite words for it —take American savers for a big ride. With inflation at 12.25 percent and the savings rate at 5.25 percent, depositors were losing 7 percent in purchasing power each and every year on the money they had entrusted to their banks. The banks, on the other hand, were borrowing our money at 5.25 percent, and at times (in 1981, for example) lending it out to their prime customers at 20.5 percent. That meant that they were making over 15 percent on our money in nominal terms, and even 8 percent in real terms, while we were losing 7 percent each year in terms of the goods and services our saved money could buy.

Worse still, rich Americans were not subject to such financial abuse. In 1973 all interest-rate ceilings for large deposits were removed. Thus people who had $100,000 or more could bypass savings accounts by buying "jumbo" certificates of deposit and get whatever rate the banks chose to pay, the same banks that were paying ordinary depositors that mandatory 5.25 percent. When the prime was 20.5 percent, the banks could still make money by offering as much as 18 percent on jumbo CDs. And they did! So the rich were getting richer from their savings, and the not-so-rich were getting—screwed.

No wonder that for decades Americans have saved less than almost any other people on earth, and as a result our production has fallen farther and farther behind Germany's and Japan's. The Germans and the Japanese save three to four times as much as we do in proportion to their disposable income, meaning that they can make vastly larger amounts of money available to industry for investment purposes, to finance automation and robotics in the automobile industry, for example. It is this savings-invest-ment-productivity process which allows the same-sized labor force in both countries to produce almost *two* cars in Japan for every *one* produced in Detroit. Since our low-productivity labor force is paid twice as much as their high-productivity one, no wonder our automotive industry almost collapsed as a result of "unfair" foreign competition.

But that's really beside the point I want to make here. Congress did not abolish Regulation Q because it was unfair and counterproductive. What did the trick was the Yankee ingenuity of a small group of financial entrepreneurs who figured out a way around Q. In retrospect, their discov-ery was elementary. What they hit upon was the idea that all somebody had to do to attract thousands of small savings accounts (eligible for only 5.25 percent at the banks) was to "bundle" these small accounts into large ones involving units of $100,000 or $1,000,000, and then take such "bundles" and invest them in those *unregulated* jumbo CDs paying 15 or 18 percent. Final step: simply pass this interest back through to the little guys after deducting—naturally—a small fee. The entrepreneurs called them money market funds.

This "discovery" took place in the early 1970's, but it took the Ameri-can public a long time to catch on. I remember that as late as 1977 I was on various television talk shows around the country discussing financial matters. I invariably suggested that the best place for people to "park" their money was just such money market funds. Most talk-show hosts had never heard of them, and some watched me with great distrust as I said they were one of the greatest discoveries since popcorn. In fact, I recall that at the end of one such program the host insisted on stressing that any investment suggestions that had been made were strictly those of Paul Erdman and should in no way be construed as representations endorsed by the network, its affiliates, subsidiaries, employees, relatives of employees or household pets of employees. Five years later, by December 1982, Americans, presumably by now including even talk-show hosts, had placed almost a *quarter of a trillion dollars* in money market funds, money for the most part yanked out of savings banks and savings and loans. For not only were the S&Ls paying just the mandatory 5.5 percent, but the whole savings and loan industry was listing dangerously, having borrowed short-term at 20 percent while its mortgage portfolio was bringing in only 8 percent. By the early 1980's even the banks' savings accounts were hemorrhaging. How could they possibly compete for savings any longer? They couldn't. So they finally fell back on the old rule: if you can't beat them, join them. The banks told their lobbyists to tell Congress to abolish Regulation Q, and the deed was done on December 14, 1982. Now the banks can pay any rate of interest they want. Overnight even the country's largest banks, including Bank of America and Citibank, jumped the savings rate to 11 percent. By then the rate of inflation was down to 3 percent. *Voilà!* We small savers were now *making* 8 percent on our money in terms of purchasing power instead of *losing* 7 percent.

Ah yes, the cynics among you are saying, but for how long? To be sure, once the banks and savings and loans had gotten a lot of their money back from those johnny-come-lately money market funds—the flow back to banks amounted to $330 billion in the four months following December 14, 1982—that 11 percent they were paying on the new money market *accounts* dropped back to 8 percent. But it stayed well above the rate of inflation, which was now 3 percent, and equally important, it stayed above the rates being offered by the money market *funds*. The banks knew that if they ever started to play games with the savers again, the now-much-smarter investing public would yank its dough out of the banks in 1984 just as quickly as it had in 1979 and go right back to the funds.

The joys of competition! What should provide even more joy is the likelihood that this new situation might last awhile.

Thanks to the competition provided by the money market funds, the interest rates we will be getting in the future will be indexed to inflation. As inflation goes up, so will the now *competitive* rates we will get from *both the banks and the funds*. If, for example, the rate of inflation in 1985 goes back up to 10 percent, general short-term lending rates will no doubt go back up to 14 or 15 percent—at least—and the rate of interest on our savings will also move up by the same proportion—to 11 or 12 percent. Why? Because it will still leave a 2 to 3 percent spread between the banks' borrowing and lending rates, making it profitable for them to compete among themselves for funds even at these now higher levels. So, finally, we can count on our money making more in terms of interest than it will be losing in purchasing power because of inflation not just today but as far as can be seen into the future. It truly makes sense for Americans to save now.

Not only that, but the December 14, 1982, change of rules also resulted in a new element of *safety*. Perhaps it was not that much *additional* safety, but still, these days you can't get too much of that particular quality. One "problem" with the money market funds is that they are not insured by any governmental agency, or by anybody else for that matter. The only institutions that get that kind of governmental protection are banks and savings and loans, although even there such insurance extends only to accounts of $100,000 or less. This leaves the funds out in the cold where insurance is concerned, since the "trick" that had made money market funds possible was that they could bypass Regulation Q by investing in jumbo CDs in excess of the $100,000 limit. Yesterday this practice left them in unregulated territory where interest rates were concerned, but today they are in uninsured territory. Not only can the funds not gain insurance protection through the banking system, but many funds have invested vast sums totally outside that system—in commercial paper, for example, paper which is nothing more than an *unsecured* IOU issued by a corporation.

No wonder, then, that when the banks were able to offer not only a higher rate of interest than the funds but also full governmental insurance coverage up to that $100,000 mark, tens upon tens of billions of dollars fled the funds and returned to the traditional banking institutions. The people who made that "return trip" made the right decision. Bank money market accounts are simply more attractive than the funds. True, you are allowed only six transactions a month where the bank accounts are concerned, whereas the funds allow an unlimited number of withdrawals. But in real life this "restriction" is meaningless. Most people use their checking accounts to pay their bills anyway. So you make two transfers a month from your money market account to your checking account in amounts roughly calculated to cover expenses and the "problem" is solved. The smartest way to operate is to make sure that your checking account is of the "Super NOW" variety, i.e., one in which *you* commit to maintaining a minimum balance of $2,500, in return for which the *bank* commits to paying you a rather substantial rate of interest—5 to 6 percent—instead of the flat zero you have been getting all your life on checking account balances.

There is absolutely no reason today for anybody to have an account at any financial institution that is not interest-bearing. By sticking with the old type of no-interest checking account, all you are doing is making a gift to the bank. Similarly, it is really dumb to keep money in savings passbook accounts, where the old ceilings of 5.25 percent for banks and 5.5 percent for savings and loans still apply. Yet, amazingly, the banks still hold around a quarter of a trillion of your dollars in such accounts, despite the myriad more attractive alternatives available at the same institution. The last guy in the world who is going to point this out to you is, of course, your banker.

What proportion of your investable funds should you keep in these money market funds/accounts? A couple of years ago a good answer would have been: damn near all you've got! First, by keeping your money there you took no capital risk: put in $10,000 on Monday and it would still be there to take back out on Friday regardless of what had happened to the stock market, the bond market, the gold market or any other market. What was beautiful was that you, as a simple, dumb individual, were then able to make more interest on what was essentially a no-risk checking account than other so-called sophisticated institutional investors could on their vast portfolios of bonds.

This was because of a highly unusual situation—one where the normal "yield curve" had been literally turned upside down.

I want to stop here very briefly and explain the "yield curve" concept because it will be *very* important for you when you decide where to put your money now, or perhaps more important, where you want your money to be a year from now.

The normal yield curve is shown in Figure 16. That curve, in fact, represents just about the way things are right now. The shorter the time until maturity, the lower the interest rate. Thus the yields on money market funds/accounts arc all bunched at the bottom left-hand side— nearest to both zero years and zero rate of interest. The farther out you go in terms of years until maturity, the higher the interest rate gets. Why? Because of risk. The risk that the entity that has borrowed your money will go broke during the next thirty years is immeasurably greater than the risk that it will be unable to repay you in thirty days: thus the greater premium to the lender—you—for taking that long-term risk, a premium that comes in the form of the higher rate of interest. At least this is how the college textbooks explain how this world works. The problem is that the world doesn't always behave the way the professors would have it.

Figure 17 shows how the yield curve looked in 1980–81. What the hell happened? In 1980–81 you could get 18 percent for money you had

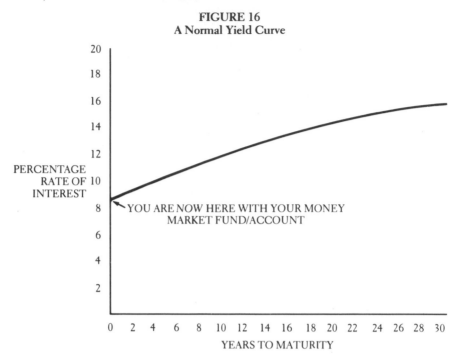

FIGURE 16
A Normal Yield Curve

committed for only a day, or a week, or a month, and those guys who had committed their money for thirty years were getting only 15 percent!

Well, what happened was a credit crunch, that's what. Everybody from General Motors to the United States government was getting short of cash. But no one wanted to commit to paying 15 percent for thirty years for the money they needed, though need it they did. Right away. So they had no qualms about paying well over that 15 percent to get it. They hoped—correctly, as it turned out—that things would return to normal in a year or two and that they could then repay expensive short-term debt by refinancing it through long-term bonds at much lower long-term rates of interest.

That explains their problem. But such circumstances resulted in a true *bonanza* for us savers and investors.

It also resulted in our getting spoiled. Normally we don't expect interest income to be very significant relative to our overall income. But look what happened when that abnormal yield curve started to develop back in 1978 (Figure 18). As you can see, the joy ride ended in 1983, and this brings us to the point: *If you agree with the pessimistic economic scenario laid out in the earlier part of this book,* you should expect a major credit crunch

FIGURE 17
An Abnormal Yield Curve

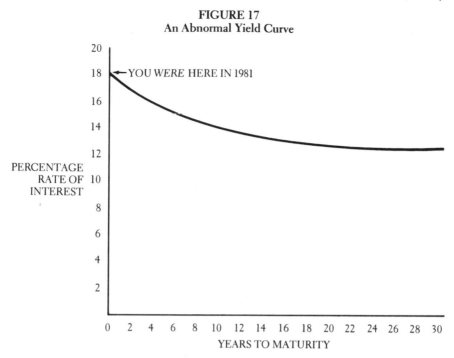

FIGURE 18
Interest Income as a Percentage of Total Personal Income

to develop again after mid-decade. That would mean that the smartest place to be with your money at that time would be either in a money market fund or in a money market account. If you feel that such a crunch

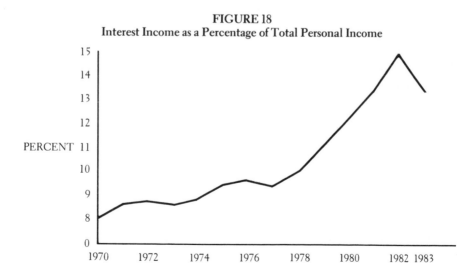

is going to come even earlier, then *it would probably be wise to keep a good percentage of your money in these accounts even today.*

Your reasoning would be this: "Sure, I'm going to 'sacrifice' some interest right now when bonds yield 12 percent and my money market account is only paying me 8 percent. But when things change, and they tend to change very, very quickly these days, my interest rate is going to start to zoom up again, while the 'suckers' who bought bonds are going to take a big bath as the price at which they can *sell* their bonds plummets well below the price they originally *paid* for them. Better safe than sorry."

My suggestion: keep at least one third of your money in either a money market fund or a money market account. If you are even the slightly nervous type, keep a lot more there. If you're *really* nervous and want the peace of mind that comes with federal insurance, choose a bank money market account.

A further thought about money market *funds;* although money market *accounts* offer a superior combination of interest and safety, a lot of people still like to stick with the funds, since they allow unlimited withdrawal and transfer privileges, or, more important, they serve as a "parking place" for cash that is between longer-term investments in other things, such as stocks or bonds. In choosing which such fund to be in, again the two factors to be considered are yield and safety. Where safety is concerned, it is generally recognized by the industry that investor losses in money funds would probably only arise in circumstances where average portfolio maturity was simply too long, e.g., where a fund was investing in ninety-day negotiable CDs or even those with maturities of one or two *years* instead of the more usual thirty-day variety. If the management of such a fund were to be caught by surprise by a sudden very sharp increase in interest rates, the value of such long-term assets could drop dramatically. A run could develop when word of this got around. The fund would have to liquidate its portfolio in order to meet the cash withdrawal demands . . . at a capital loss. And you, dear depositor, would then get back a lot less money than you had originally deposited.

Another conceivable risk arises where a fund is highly committed to investments in the CDs of offshore banks and/or in commercial paper. Such funds provide higher yields because such investments involve higher risks. In this age of credit crunches and Mexican bank debts, one should ask whether that extra 1 percent is really worth it. For chronic worriers, the *safest* type of fund is one that invests exclusively in United States government securities, and one that has an average portfolio maturity of thirty days or less. The Institute for Econometric Research in Fort Lauderdale, Florida, rates funds by taking into account all these factors. Capital Preservation Funds I and II, which invest exclusively in short-maturity government paper, consistently get the top ratings . . . but also provide some of the lowest yields.

As usual, you won't get something for nothing.

Chapter 13

oᴑooᴑooᴑo

Bonds

IF MONEY MARKET ACCOUNTS are a sure thing, and money market funds very close to it, bonds definitely are not . . . especially in the *long* run.

The short run might be something else. Whether you prefer my pessimistic or my optimistic scenario concerning our economic future, the attractiveness of bonds as an investment in the *immediate* future will not really differ, because these two roads will more or less *overlap* in the short run. Whether you are an optimist or a pessimist, 1984 is going to be one of continuing growth, but more important where bonds are concerned, it may also be a year of relatively low rates of inflation and of relatively steady rates of interest . . . one hopes!

Bond markets sustain themselves well in such circumstances. When interest rates fall, bond prices rise, and even when bond prices do no more than hold steady, you still get a return on your invested money (11–13 percent) which is very good compared to what you can get from either your money market fund or your money market account when the yield curve is still "normal," as it is likely to remain this side of a major credit crunch. If you have to sell your bonds a year from now, the odds are good that you will still get 100 percent of your invested capital back.

Bonds become disasters when interest rates take off suddenly. For when *interest rates* rise, *bond prices* fall. Why is that? Now, I don't want to sound "elementary," but I have some friends who *still* can't figure it out, and this explanation is for them.

A lot of people who bought bonds in the mid-1970's and got clobbered as a result can explain it all too lucidly. Typically, an investor purchased a newly issued 10 percent thirty-year bond in 1975 for $1,000. In essence he "bought" himself $100 a year interest. Six years later newly issued thirty-year bonds were yielding 15 percent. For $1,000 you could now "buy" yourself $150 a year interest. Those *new* bond *yields* set the market standard for the *prices* of all *old* bonds. All *old* bonds now had to be repriced in line with the now prevailing 15 percent. Thus in 1981 in order to "buy" $100 a year in interest, an investor had to put out only $670 dollars. Right? $670 × 15 percent = $100. So if in 1981 you had had to sell that 10 percent bond for which you paid $1,000 in 1975, you would have gotten precisely that price: $670 instead of the $1,000 you had originally paid for that piece of paper six years earlier. You would have lost 33 percent of your capital.

Not too smart. Lesson: if you expect interest rates to rise in the near future, don't buy bonds.

The problem is that interest rates, especially long-term interest rates, tended to move within a very narrow band and to move very slowly within that narrow band. But that was in the old days. Now it's anyone's guess where interest rates are likely to be five, ten or twenty years out.

FIGURE 19
Interest Rates Throughout U.S. History

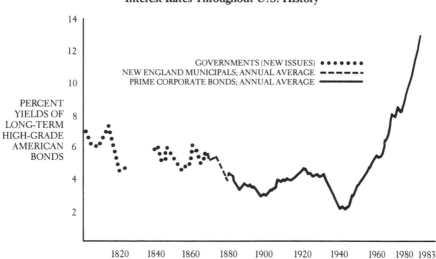

Figure 19 shows that between 1860 and 1965—105 years!—bond interest rates never moved above 6 percent and were only below 3 percent for about a decade between the late 1930's and the late 1940's. Since then they have gone from 6 percent to 15 percent and then down to 12 percent within the eighteen years between 1965 and 1983. Lesson Number two:

you'd make a big mistake to buy bonds, stick them in the vault and forget them. You have to be prepared to move in and out just as you normally would be prepared to do with stocks. Remember, diamonds aren't forever. Neither are bonds.

How does an average private investor involve himself in the bond market?

You can buy a bond as easily as you can buy a stock. Just call up your broker. However, if you do so and say you want to buy $10,000 worth of AT&T bonds, he is going to be very, very bored. He'll do it for you, but it will probably cost more than it's worth either to him or to you. For bonds are usually traded in $250,000, $1 million or $10 million lots. The market is dominated by institutions—banks and pension funds. It takes just as much time for your broker to do a $10 million deal as it does to process your $10,000 one. The odds are that once your broker has bought the bonds you asked for, he will put them in your account and promptly forget about them—forever.

Furthermore, if you insist on doing your own thing in bonds, you should realize that you are going to pay a price. To put it bluntly, you really get taken for a ride when you try to liquidate small positions in the bond market, and small positions are generally regarded as those involving "odd lots" of less than $250,000. Thus if you have laboriously put together a portfolio of, for example, a dozen corporate bonds with a face value of $1,000 each, when you try to sell out, you will find a spread (the difference between the buying and selling price) of as much as $40 or $50.

Finally, and it happens so often it is hard to believe: individuals buy, or are *sold*, bonds that they think are due first in thirty years, ensuring that a high rate of interest will be locked in for the duration. Then they find out that the fine print gives the issuer the right to call the bond after only five years by paying a tiny premium. The problem is that it is not that easy to spot such bonds, loaded in the issuers' favor, since they sell at essentially the same prices and offer essentially the same yields as bonds without such call provisions. Furthermore, where individual investors are concerned, the bond salesman might be the last guy to point all this out.

The smart way to go is with a bond fund where somebody knows exactly what he is buying and then *continues* to mind the store—the store in which you now have invested your money. Because of the extreme volatility to which bond prices are now subject, this, in my judgment, is a *sine qua non* for private investing in *long-term* fixed interest securities in the 1980's. But be careful *what kind* of fund, for there are two types —the right kind and the wrong kind.

Alas, most bond funds are of the wrong kind. They are organized in the form of "unit trusts." All the managements of these "funds" do is collect money from tens of thousands of small investors, just as the managers of money market funds do, but instead of buying thirty-day CDs, they buy bonds first due in twenty or twenty-five years. Then they stand pat. You have bought yourself a piece—a unit—of a very, very long-term investment portfolio that will remain essentially unchanged for the duration. If long-term bond prices collapse again, it will be up to *you* to sense that the worst is about to return and to get out before it's too late. Unless you buy, lock, stock and barrel, the "optimistic'" economic scenario summarized by Figure 15 on page 106, where inflation holds steady in the 3–4 percent range during the next three to four, possibly seven to eight, years, and where both long- and short-term interest rates steadily decline over that same period, stay away from unit trust bond funds. And stay away, for sure, from trying to put together your own portfolio of bonds by buying $5,000 of AT&T here and $10,000 of Florida Power & Light there, for you will very probably take a licking both on price and on commission (spread) when the time comes to bail out.

The way to go instead is with bond *funds,* or income funds, as they are also called, which do your thinking for you. The manager of such a fund does not simply buy a portfolio of bonds and then lock them up and forget about them. If the manager feels that long-term interest rates are about to take off, he dumps his portfolio and reinvests the proceeds in securities with very much shorter maturities. In essence, he converts his bond fund into a near equivalent of a money market fund. This approach makes sense especially where municipal bonds are concerned. There the "switch" would involve selling fifteen-year tax-free bonds and replacing them with one-year tax-free notes. Because of this flexibility, and because of the extraordinary yields available to heavily taxed citizens, I think that municipal bond funds of this type represent a solid investment, almost tailor-made for people who make at least $45,000 a year. If you are in the top tax bracket—i.e., if you will have to pay 40–50 percent federal income tax on any *more* money you might earn, and if you live in California or New York, for instance, where the state will hit you for an extra 11 percent on top of that 50 percent—the yields available on municipals are almost *irresistible.* A fund that pays around 9.5 percent tax free is the equivalent of a taxable bond that pays almost 20 percent, although there is no such animal as a highly rated 20 percent bond, or anything close to it. The extraordinary yields offered by municipal bond funds in my opinion more than compensate for the possibility that the manager of your fund might make some bad decisions, such as betting that interest rates will go down when, in fact, they are headed up, and losing 20 percent of your capital in the process. But if making money were easy, we'd all be rich, wouldn't we?

Who offers such funds? The Kemper Group in Chicago; the Franklin Group in California; Merrill Lynch, Prudential-Bache, Dean Witter, Shearson/American Express in New York and Pennsylvania; Nuveen for such states as Massachusetts, Michigan, Minnesota. Everybody is getting into the game because, I guess, it makes good sense for a lot of people with a lot of money.

Now I should add one final word: a lot of you probably *have* bonds. Well, don't panic just because you are on your own in a world that always seems to zig left just after you've zagged right. In fact, if you bought them a few years ago, you have made a lot of money in the meantime—at least on paper—resulting from the substantial increases in bond prices right across the board, which started in the summer of 1982. Well, that joy ride may be over, but the time has not yet come when interest rates will rise to such high levels that the prices of your bonds will sink below your original cost. So hang on for a while. During the next year or so your neighbor will be getting 8 percent from his money market fund while you will be getting the equivalent of double that return on your tax-free bonds. But unless you are a committed optimist, you ought to start to get nervous around mid-decade when the deficit/debt problem might begin to catch up with us. Should this begin to happen, signaling that the pessimistic scenario is starting to phase in ahead of my schedule, meaning that the four variables—M1, inflation, growth and interest rates, especially interest rates—collectively begin moving in directions that are disastrous for bonds, you ought to start preparing to get out early in 1985 before all those paper capital gains you made since mid-1982 start to go down the drain again.

Chapter 14

oᴑooᴑooᴑo

Government
Securities

F IVE OR TEN YEARS AGO in a book like this I would not even have
mentioned government securities where individual investors were concerned. When I was in banking in Switzerland, we put money into darn
near every kind of investment available in the entire *world* for our clien-
tele, but I don't remember one single instance when we ever bought a
T-bill, a T-note or a T-bond for a customer, or for our own account for
that matter. The closest we ever came was to buy World Bank bonds
issued in Switzerland and denominated in Swiss francs. And we did that
not because of the "governmental" aspect of the issuer, but rather because
it was a good way for foreign clients to buy Swiss francs and actually get
some interest on them. As you know, or perhaps don't know because
you've never banked in Switzerland, when you make a deposit with a Swiss
bank, the bank promises to pay you a mini-rate of interest—say 3 percent,
or even 4 percent if they are eager—but by the time all the foreign
exchange costs, the endless fees and the 30 percent tax withholding are
deducted, you almost always end up earning nothing whatsoever on your
money. On World Bank bonds at least you got 5 percent or even 6
percent, and you actually *received* the interest intact. But even that did
not please everybody.

I personally used to take care of a client who was a big-wig scientist on
the West Coast and expected us to make a lot of money for him in
Switzerland. It was back in 1970, I think, that I decided to put about
$50,000 or so of his money into Swiss franc bonds under a discretionary
management power that we had over his account. When he got the notice

of the transaction he screamed blue murder. Why did he need a Swiss bank to put him into 5 percent bonds when even the dumbest broker in San Francisco could get him 7 percent on Pacific Gas & Electric bonds? Because, I tried to explain, the Swiss franc was going to go way up relative to the dollar. And when it was time to sell that World Bank bond for him in a few years, and convert the proceeds back into dollars, he might very well have doubled his dollars. He failed to grasp that, so instead we bought him some silver futures and he lost his shirt.

But that's not the point. At that time *nobody* considered, much less discussed the fact, that government securities were *safe,* and that for this reason alone they might merit consideration for investment purposes. Well, no more. I get an average of 2.6 callers during each radio program I do in San Francisco asking me whether or not they should "roll over their T-bills," whether they should maybe "go out a bit and get into T-notes," and "Do you think that it might be smart to go downtown to the Federal Reserve Bank and buy them directly instead of going through a broker or bank, thus saving the commission?" The answer I always give to the last is yes.

Safety is a quality that's very hard to define. We've got services in the United States—Moody's and Standard and Poor's—that examine everything from the balance sheets to the managements of corporations and then give a rating, indicating *relative* safety where securities are concerned. The safest rating is AAA where Standard and Poor's is concerned, and Aaa under Moody's rating system, meaning that the company is going to remain solvent eternally and pay you the interest due you on your bonds forever. When your bonds get down to C, the company that issued them is just this side of Chapter 11 and your bond is just a prayer away from default. If you have a bond that is assigned a D, you have probably seen the last of *that* money.

Now, we were all taught at our grandmother's knee that the safest investments in the private sector in the entire *world* were AT&T bonds. Right? Wrong. In the middle of March 1983 Moody's decided that because the Bell System was split up by the geniuses in charge of antitrust, the company was no longer the Rock of Gibraltar and the bonds that AT&T had been issuing over the years and decades to the trusting public —all $47 *billion* of them, the cumulative total resulting from the fact that Ma Bell bonds have for decades represented 10 percent of *all* corporate bonds marketed each year in the entire United States—were not a dead cert after all. AT&T bonds were dropped one notch down the safety scale to Aa1, but some of the bonds of other former Bell units, such as Michigan Bell, were dropped *six* notches.

Or take the "Whoops" bonds, those issued by the Washington Public Power Supply System. If AT&T was the largest corporate issuer of bonds in the United States, WPPSS was this country's largest issuer of tax-exempt bonds, and like Ma Bell's, almost all of its bonds were given the top rating, triple-A, by the major credit rating agencies. Well, wrong again! As everybody now knows, the bonds were issued to finance the construction of five huge nuclear power plants in the Northwest. Construction costs were originally budgeted at $4 billion. By 1982 the cost of completion was reestimated at $24 billion. Plants 4 and 5 were cancelled, and the $2.25 billion in bonds issued to finance them were defaulted upon; completion of plants 1 and 2 is in doubt and the bond issues for them are now also of doubtful value. Standard and Poor's was forced to suspend its ratings on all of these issues that the public had widely—but mistakenly—thought were backed by government guarantees. For they had been told that a federal agency, the Bonneville Power Administration, was involved, carrying with it, one thought, an implied federal guarantee. Furthermore, as an irate bondholder wrote in a letter to the *Wall Street Journal*, "Whoops is a 'municipal corporation of the state of Washington.' That phrase is used on the face of the bonds. Investors purchase revenue authority bonds because states have a moral obligation to back up bonds issued within their borders."

So much for both implied and moral obligations. And perhaps also so much for public utilities as sound investments. On December 1, 1983, the *Wall Street Journal* started off its lead story with the following words: "The electric-utility industry, jolted by the 1979 accident at Three Mile Island and wounded by the Washington Public Power Supply System's 1983 default, is poised on the edge of a new nuclear crisis. Huge nuclear power plants, long overdue and far above budget, threaten to overwhelm the utilities that are building them."

"Nobody ever thought a municipality could go bankrupt until it happened to Cleveland," Paul R. Bjorn, a utility expert with Price Waterhouse & Co., the accounting company, told the *Journal*, and he went on to say that the once inconceivable prospect of a utility company's going into bankruptcy proceedings is "an increasing possibility." Irving Bupp, a specialist in utility financing at the Harvard Business School, put it another way: "Nuclear plants are being built on giant Master-Cards."

It would seem to me that in light of all this, any of you out there who are invested in public utilities would be well advised to check out how deeply committed your particular company is to nuclear power. When you get the answer, you may very well conclude that your money will be a whole lot safer if you sell your utilities and use the proceeds to buy government notes or bonds.

Public utilities are just another in a long string of similar disappointments. First hundreds of S&L's all around the country, but especially in California, were going broke and being rescued at the last minute through government-sponsored forced mergers with larger institutions. Then came the Drysdale Securities affair in New York, which cost the big banks there a couple of hundred million because their government securities traders were too careless in their dealings with a small and obscure firm that was gambling with a bond inventory that it did not exactly own. Then followed the collapse of the Penn Square Bank, which showed that banks as far away as Seafirst in Seattle, or Continental Illinois in Chicago, had bought hundreds of millions of dollars' worth of uncollectable oil-exploration loans from a two-bit bank in Oklahoma City, sold to them by a "banker" whose show-stopper was drinking beer out of his cowboy boots. Then came the sudden revelations that some of the country's largest banks had lent somewhere between half and all of their capital and reserves to a bankrupt nation south of the Rio Grande.

The effect of all this has been that a lot of Americans have lost faith in the solidity of traditional financial institutions. For the first time in their lives, a lot of Americans, and not just crazies, truly fear that their banks might go broke and that they, as a result, could be left stranded outside the door with their life's savings gone—just like their mothers or grandfathers in the mid-1930's. They all know about the FDIC and the FSLIC, but they have also been told that these insurance corporations are ridiculously undercapitalized relative to the risks that prevail. There's no way to convince them that while the FDIC has only $11 billion, Congress could increase that reserve fund by any amount it chose and probably would do just that literally overnight in an emergency. They hear, but they don't believe.

What has resulted is a type of invisible capital flight, a flight from the *relative* safety of the banks and AT&T bonds into what is considered the *absolute* safety of United States government securities, especially those that have very short maturities, such as ninety-day Treasury bills.

Well, when T-bills were yielding 15 percent, why not? But I don't think it makes a whole lot of sense to buy T-bills when you can get essentially the same rate of interest on a governmentally insured deposit at your bank, plus the convenience of having your money just a phone call away; or much higher interest on notes issued by either Fannie Mae (the Federal National Mortgage Association, or FNMA) or Ginnie Mae (the Government National Mortgage Association, or GNMA), agencies which finance mortgages and which are backed by a federal government guarantee; or 9–10 percent *tax-free* from a properly managed municipal bond fund. The end is certainly not *that* near!

What might make sense for insecure investors are Treasury notes, especially during those periodic "up-blips" in medium-term interest rates. Strike fast when such blips come (and you can, since such notes are auctioned every two weeks) and you can then lock in both a reasonably high yield for the next couple of years—often almost two full percentage points above yields available on T-bills or on deposits in money market accounts—and enjoy the "absolute" safety of a security backed 100 percent by the full faith and credit of the United States of America. You should plan to hold such notes until maturity—two years is hardly a long time—when you are *absolutely* sure of getting all your capital back, *regardless* of what has happened to interest rates in the meantime. The minimum denomination of such notes is $5,000; interest is paid every six months, and is free of state income taxes. Any bank will buy them for you and keep them for you, for a very small fee.

For those of you whose prime aim is capital *preservation*—and in my judgment that should be the special aim of anybody over fifty-five whose personal earning powers are starting to wane and who must depend on the survival of his or her capital for personal survival—this type of investment is, I think, consistent with a prudent view of our economic future. Fixed-interest securities are good investments in times of low rates of inflation and relatively stable interest rates. I expect just such conditions to prevail during 1984 and, perhaps, the initial months of 1985. Thereafter—who knows? If by then inflation returns as a disrupting, though not necessarily dominant, force in our lives, you will be nicely liquid—just when those two-year T-notes mature.

If you want a very easy-to-read booklet on government securities—everything you wanted to know and more—just write to:

The Federal Reserve Bank of Richmond
Bank and Public Relations Department
P.O. Box 27622
Richmond, Virginia 23261

Ask for "Buying Treasury Securities at Federal Reserve Banks." It's free.

Chapter 15

o☉oo☉oo☉o

Gold

A LL RIGHT: enough of this conservative stuff. And as long as we are taking a leap into risky territory, why not start right off with precious metals—gold (discussed in this chapter) and silver (see Chapter 16).

Gold to me is one of the most fascinating subjects in the world. This metal has been at the core of monetary systems from the very beginning of recorded history, and probably for a long time before. That is why Keynes could correctly refer to it as a "barbarous relic." Following that lead, a large body of academics, especially in the United States, fervently wishes that gold would go away, allowing "rational" management of our monetary affairs to finally prevail forevermore.

Well, their wish came true in 1971 when President Nixon closed the gold window, breaking the link between the dollar and gold, and thus also breaking the link between *all* currencies and gold. "Rational" monetary management has prevailed ever since and has given the world one of the wildest inflationary rides in centuries. That very disappointing track record, plus the fact that the key nations of the world—starting with the United States and the Soviet Union, but extending to Britain, France, Germany and Switzerland—all have a major vested interest in gold simply because they all own vast amounts of that metal (Western European governments own 423 million ounces; the U.S. 264 million) assures us that barbarous as it might appear, gold is going to remain a very special type of "commodity" well into the third millennium after Christ.

Gold is where governmental monetary interests and private investment interests overlap in a unique way, which is why for the last century or so, gold has been among the worst investments around. For most of the past century, governments have kept the price of gold absolutely constant so that for individual investors *anything* was better than gold, an asset that neither yielded any interest nor provided any capital appreciation. Consider this: between 1879 and 1934 the price of gold remained at exactly $20.67 an ounce. In 1934 it was jumped to $35 an ounce by U.S. government fiat and stayed there for another thirty-four years, i.e., until 1968.

Between 1879 and 1968 an opportunity to make money on gold occurred but once, in the early 1930's, when the price moved to $35 an ounce, and this was at a time when everybody was so broke that very few people were able to take advantage of it.

Erdman's rule number one for investing in gold, therefore, is: Don't do it if the world is on any sort of gold "standard," since it means not just fighting city hall, but fighting the White House, No. 10 Downing Street, the Swiss National Bank, the Russians and every other government on earth. That's not smart.

Knowing that, nevertheless, I (that is, my Swiss bank—both for itself and for its customers) started to invest heavily in gold in 1967 even though it meant that in essence I was going against just such overwhelming vested governmental interests in maintaining that $35 an ounce forever. Why? Because in that year it became apparent that the post-1934 gold price, or more specifically, the post–World War II global monetary system based on $35-an-ounce gold, was beginning to unravel.

The first symptom of this was the forced devaluation of the pound sterling in October 1967. Our bank had taken a massive short position in that currency. Why? Because British costs and prices had moved way out of line with those of the rest of the world, the result of the cost-push inflation promoted by England's irresponsible labor unions, an inflation that was further fueled by increases in money supply furnished by an accommodating Bank of England. As a result, British goods could no longer compete in the world with sterling valued at $2.80. Imports soared, exports died and England's balances of trade and payments were deeply and increasingly in deficit, which meant that massive amounts of sterling were pouring out into the rest of the world. The point had been reached where either the government would have to undermine the unions by creating a credit crunch, forcing the country into recession, thus creating unemployment and an end to the cost-push inflationary process, or it could simply let things continue to go as they were at home and forget about sterling at $2.80.

It chose the latter and devalued sterling to $2.40, with the result that not only did our bank make out like gangbusters, but we asked ourselves whether the dollar could be far behind. For in 1967 Johnson's programs for providing guns for Vietnam and butter for the American masses without raising taxes were now at full blast. An inflation like Britain's simply *had* to result. Then the key question for America would be the same as it had been for Britain: would it be *worth* it to defend the dollar? For England in 1967 the defense of its currency would have meant borrowing billions of dollars in order to buy up all the sterling that was being sold by speculators like ourselves who were making a "run" on the currency. Britain decided that mortgaging its future for the sake of that $2.80 simply wasn't worth it.

The question for the United States would be different. It could not devalue if the rest of the world lost faith in the dollar because, as we have already seen and as silly as it sounds, nobody in Washington knew how to do it. The only parity that Washington could defend, or *change*, was that which linked the dollar to gold at $35 an ounce. The pledge to maintain that link was what made the dollar "good as gold." Therefore if a run on the dollar developed, what would happen is that for every $35 any central bank in the rest of the world wanted to cash in, the United States would have to give in return one ounce of gold from Fort Knox. To stop this, the smart money crowd in Switzerland reasoned, the United States would simply jack up the price of gold. In other words, a "gold window of opportunity," similar to that which had opened up prior to 1934 for the only time in over half a century, seemed to be about to open once more.

The window opened, all right, but not until four years later. In the summer of 1971 the French government led the drive on Fort Knox, which panicked Nixon & Co. Within days, as we have seen, Nixon suspended gold sales. The result was the end of dollar/gold convertibility and of government intervention in the gold market aimed at holding the price at any given level. For the first time in the twentieth century, gold was free to find its "equilibrium" level.

It didn't take much to figure out that this level was a hell of a lot higher than $35 an ounce. The price of every commodity on earth had risen many-fold since 1934, the last time the gold price had been adjusted. It was now just a matter of how far gold would go up, and how fast.

The era of massive, violent global speculation in gold had dawned. The gold-bugs went nuts. The process finally peaked in early 1980 when the price hit $875 an ounce, a twenty-five-fold increase in price—what you might call an overcorrection.

By 1983 gold had "settled" down in the $350–$400 range after briefly bottoming out earlier at below $300.

What now?

One problem with discussing gold is that it seems to bring out the worst in people. Either they hate it—regard it as a "sterile" investment, i.e., one that does nothing to benefit society, and regard anybody who invests in it as essentially unpatriotic, since real Americans should be buying the stock of Chrysler Corporation and getting America going again—or they see gold as a panacea which will solve all of mankind's problems provided we return to a "gold standard." It is left unsaid that a return to gold might also solve a lot of the gold-bugs' personal financial problems if the new gold/dollar link were established at, say, $1,000 an ounce.

The time and place to meet the gung-ho gold-bugs is New Orleans in October. As many as ten thousand of them gather for their annual get-together, to hear speeches denouncing all political leaders as traitors to the middle class and servants of the Trilateral Commission. Gold and only gold will bring the rascals back in line and save the world from imminent, and I mean *imminent,* financial collapse. I gave a speech there once—in 1981—suggesting that lower inflation, lower interest rates, lower gold prices and ultimately good times were just around the corner. I've not been invited back.

They prefer speakers who suggest that runaway inflation combined with a depression deeper than that of the 1930's is what lies around that corner, not good times, and they especially want to be told that where the price of gold is concerned, even the sky won't be the limit. They are always in search of a new leader who will outbid the last one. Their latest favorite —no, favorites, plural—are two ladies from—get this—San José, Costa Rica, the Aden sisters. These female gold gurus, who as far as I know neither sing nor play the guitar, have spotted and charted the gold "up-trend line" since that first breakout from $35 in 1968. It is shown in Figure 20.

Naturally, they have projected this trend into the murky future, and I think you have already guessed what their conclusion is: yes—the line will continue onward and upward. As they recently stated in their newsletter, *The Aden Analysis,* "it is quite possible that inflation could reach a peak at approximately the 25% level by 1985–86. Considering the gold market, our research still indicates that for these and other technical reasons [!] gold could ultimately reach the $3,700–$4,400 level in the same period."

FIGURE 20
The Gold Price

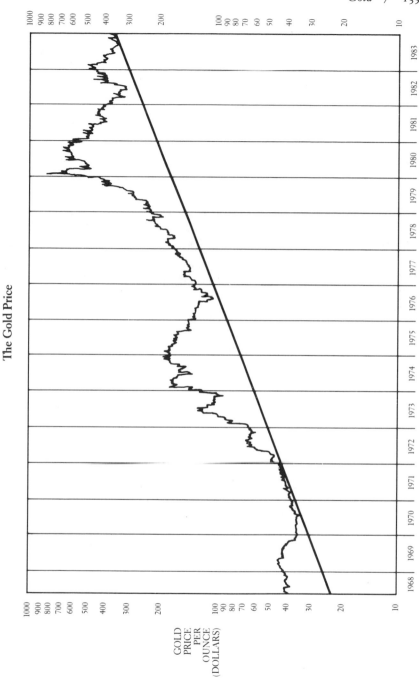

GOLD
PRICE
PER
OUNCE
(DOLLARS)

At the last New Orleans conference the Aden sisters were the big hit!

This is, of course, utter nonsense. And paradoxically, if the gold-bugs actually got their wish—a return to that undefined gold standard for which they yearn—the result would be that when the government got actively back into the gold game and fixed and then maintained the gold price at *whatever* level, then all their fun would be over, just as it was for fifty-five years after 1879 and for thirty-four years after 1934. Such a move would break that Aden trend line more than just a little south of that $4,400 mark, and we would go back to the dull old days of a fixed price.

To summarize: I wouldn't count on a return-to-the-gold-standard scenario any more than I would on those ladies who have shown the way from San José. We are going to see no return to any gold standard in this decade. How could the United States possibly finance those $200 billion deficits looming ahead under a gold standard? Answer: it couldn't. How could the world "manage" its way out of the Third World debt crisis under a gold standard? Answer: it couldn't. So forget about it.

Now *if* the U.S. government is *not* going to refix the price of gold, and *if*, in the absence of that, the gold price is *not* going to $4,400 an ounce by 1986, what is a good guess as to what it *is* going to do?

I think we can develop a fairly logical answer to that, with the help of an analysis done by Dr. Horace W. Brock. He has a Ph.D. in mathematics from Princeton, where he was a student of John von Neumann, one of the leading mathematicians of our century, whose greatest contributions were to probability (game) theory. Brock now runs his own think tank in California, Strategic Economic Decisions, which sums up exactly what he helps people make. Anglo American Corporation—the De Beers group, which is almost as heavy in gold as it is in diamonds—commissioned him to figure out where the gold price is headed. By chance I sat beside him at dinner one night in San Francisco recently and came away convinced that he probably has as good a fix on gold's future as anybody. He uses the year 1987 as his "target" year.

He has determined that everybody, but everybody, who has a vested interest in gold and has some brains as well seems to agree that it is *investment* demand for gold (in contrast to demand for gold by consumers who actually *use* it, such as the electronics or jewelry industries) that will ultimately determine the price, and that there will be five critical determinants of that demand in 1987:

> the level of political tension, which he describes as the "world anxiety coefficient"

· real economic growth rates, especially in the United States, Europe, Japan and Southeast Asia

· the rate of inflation in non-Communist industrialized countries

· real rates of interest, particularly those in the United States and Europe

· the relative strength of the U.S. dollar

Brock is basically keeping his eye on the same variables that I have suggested *you* follow—interest rates, inflation and growth—although he leaves out money supply. Maybe they don't believe in monetarist theories at Princeton. In any case, depending on the forecasts you make concerning these key determinants, you can decide whether or not to buy gold as an investment.

The bad-for-gold scenario, under which few people will buy gold for investment purposes, would involve the following conditions:

1. Low inflation
2. High real interest rates
3. Low real economic growth
4. Low levels of political tension
5. A strong U.S. dollar

In other words, except for item 3, the conditions that prevail as I write. If you accept the optimistic view of the *immediate* future—1984–85— probably items 1, 4 and 5 on the bad-for-gold scenario will remain unchanged, while real interest rates will fall and economic growth rates will remain at a moderately high level. To this extent, the prospects for gold will improve marginally.

But on balance, I think one would have to conclude that gold would be a *bad* investment should such "optimistic" conditions prevail during the next three or four years. If Reaganomics succeeds, then the man the gold-bugs used to revere most, namely Mr. Reagan, will have turned out to be their worst enemy.

Conversely, if you are looking for good-for-gold conditions, they would be these:

1. High inflation
2. Low real interest rates
3. High real economic growth (since investors are then richer and could more easily afford a position in gold).
4. High levels of political tension
5. A weak U.S. dollar

If we compare this list with our pessimistic scenario, we get at least three out of five, i.e., items 1, 2 and 5 (with 2 a little iffy), 4 a maybe and 3 a no-show.

Let's narrow it down still further, leaving Brock aside for the moment. It used to be that people bought gold so as not to *lose* money. This made sense even during those long periods when gold was fixed at either $20.67 an ounce or $35 an ounce, *if* you were about to become a refugee from Eastern or Central Europe in the 1920's or 1930's and wanted a portable and anonymous means by which you could take what was left of your wealth with you, or if you were a Brazilian in the 1950's trying to escape the ravages of hyperinflation. Gold, then, was a hedge against *losing* money.

Things are quite different now. Today the "world anxiety coefficient" still plays a role, but, for the time being, it's relatively small. The *Wall Street Journal* tracked the anxiety "effect" on gold during the first two years of this decade, and detected diminishing returns where bad news was concerned:

Rumor of Soviet invasion of Iran, January 1980	+$87.00
Pessimistic report on hostages, April 1980	+$34.40
Rumor that Iranians had seized Soviet embassy, July 1980	+$25.00
Reagan shot, March 1981	+$12.90
Sadat killed, October 1981	+$16.40
Martial law in Poland, December 1981	+$ 6.80
Soviets shoot down Korean airliner, September 1983	+$ 1.25
Marines massacred in Beirut, U.S. invades Grenada, October 1983	−$11.50

Hyperinflation continues to play a role today, since there is still enough of it around in Latin America and other places. And today there is a new type of "fear element" at work in the world, not related to political or war risks. If Brazil were to go into de jure default on the $90 billion it owes the world's banks, gold would probably rise by $100 in three days. But Brazil will not be pushed into default by its creditors. If it were, then the global banking system would be threatened and so would our economic well-being. Since we cannot afford to let such a thing happen, it will not. As long as the political will to prevent such default exists as it now certainly does, then there is no question that the means can be found to fund the Brazils of the world indefinitely. Therefore, although rumors of war, revolution and default will no doubt continue to cause sometimes violent short-term fluctuations in the gold price as investors try to protect themselves, the prime motivation for people to invest in gold today is not to find protection but to *make* money.

So how do you make money in gold today? Some short-term speculators track Soviet sales of gold and, depending on whether the Russians are selling or not, make their moves, but it is next to impossible to know what the Soviets are doing in the gold market in any given week or month, since most of their operations are run out of Switzerland. This means that you have to face not only the Soviet penchant for secrecy but also the Swiss bankers' penchant for the same. Anybody who claims to have cracked *that* wall of secrecy is kidding you. And even if anybody could, in the long run the information he passed on to investors would be meaningless. The Russians continue to need dollars desperately to buy everything from Canadian wheat to German machine tools. To raise those dollars, they will continue to sell all the gold they can possibly produce. The same holds true of South Africa. That country is now in a constant state of siege, at least in the minds of its leaders. South Africa must also sell all the gold it can mine to buy everything from oil for its strategic reserve to tanks and helicopters for its immense defense establishment.

So the key to making money in gold is not to watch the *supply* side. It is very predictable. *Demand* is the key variable.

Most people recognize that the key to assessing future demand, which will in turn fundamentally affect the price of gold, is the correct and early diagnosis of where inflation is headed. If gold costs $400 an ounce, and you think inflation will jump from 4 percent now to 9 percent a couple of years from now, the chances are good that gold will rise. As more and more people start catching on to where we are headed and start getting out of cash or financial assets (such as bonds) and into gold, the price will zoom up yet again. Whoever gets there first will reap the greatest profits from this process.

Back to Brock: he has put all the calculations about gold supply and demand and his guesses on the political risk coefficient and so forth into his computer and come up with a handy-dandy gold guide for the future. (Figure 21). It links the 1987 price of gold to that key determinant of its price, namely the various rates of inflation that *could* prevail in the meantime, and then assigns a probability factor to each specific forecast.

I will buy an average rate of inflation in the 1982–87 period of 4.5 percent (lower now, higher later) and thus a "calculated" price of around $700 in 1987, less a 15 percent discount based on "intuition." In summary, I go for $600.

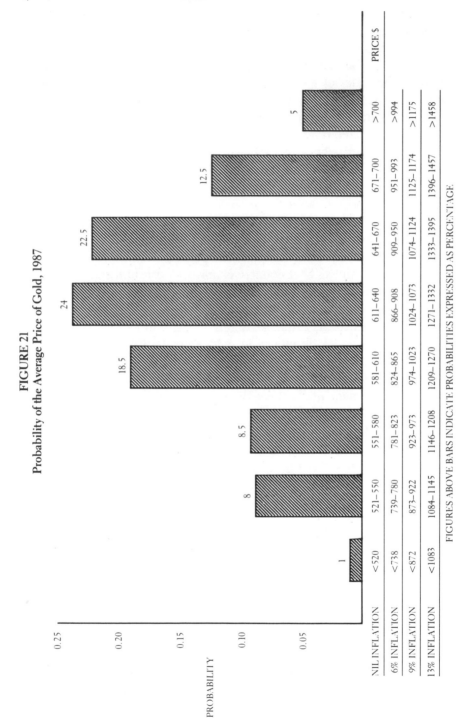

FIGURE 21
Probability of the Average Price of Gold, 1987

									PRICE $
NIL INFLATION	<520	521–550	551–580	581–610	611–640	641–670	671–700	>700	
6% INFLATION	<738	739–780	781–823	824–865	866–908	909–950	951–993	>994	
9% INFLATION	<872	873–922	923–973	974–1023	1024–1073	1074–1124	1125–1174	>1175	
13% INFLATION	<1083	1084–1145	1146–1208	1209–1270	1271–1332	1333–1395	1396–1457	>1458	

FIGURES ABOVE BARS INDICATE PROBABILITIES EXPRESSED AS PERCENTAGE

Why? Why not $4,400 an ounce, as the Aden sisters project?

Because, as I have already mentioned, I simply cannot buy the pessimistic assumptions upon which such gold price forecasts are based, namely 25 percent rates of inflation in the United States as early as in 1985–86. All such forecasts of almost runaway inflation, and the very high gold prices that such inflation would evoke, are based upon runaway growth in this nation's money supply. They take the growth of M1 (the hot "transactional" money in the system), which was growing at a rate well into double digits between August 1982 and June 1983, and project that such rates will rise ever higher and faster into the future. Well, that's not happening, and with Paul Volcker still running the Federal Reserve, it is not going to happen. Moreover, the economy, the *real* economy, is still growing at a fairly good clip. Thus as I write, the *difference* between the rate of real economic growth and the rate of increase in the money supply is *narrowing,* not widening dramatically as the pessimists have been forecasting. Furthermore, we *still* have enormous slack in the system in the form of gravely underutilized plant and labor capacity, slack which acts as a deterrent to the revival of inflation in the cost-push sense. Therefore, I do *not* believe that a base is being built today for tomorrow's 25 percent rate of inflation and a gold price that is double, triple, or ten times current levels.

So what about gold at $250 an ounce, a price level that would probably be compatible with the optimistic scenario?

I don't buy that either. For I *do* believe that in spite of Volcker's best efforts, the growth of the money supply has been and still is excessive. I also believe that as the economy continues to revive, we will see bottlenecks in the production process and a revival of excessive demands from the labor unions. Furthermore, world commodity prices seem be on the go again. They bottomed out in 1982 and have been rising ever since— up 25 percent on average already. Food prices were one of the keys to the rise of inflation in the United States in the 1970's, an inflation triggered to a substantial degree by excessive sales of wheat to the Soviet Union, creating a shortage here at home. The combination of renewed sales to Russia, crop damage suffered in 1983 as a result of heat and drought, and the massive reduction in land under cultivation evoked by Reagan's PIK (Payment-in-Kind) program might have the same impact starting in 1984–85. All these factors will lead to a rising rate of inflation. I do not think that Volcker will dare choke off this revival by once again throttling further growth in the money supply, evoking very high interest rates, which would cause an abrupt abortion of the recovery, and once again soaring unemployment rates. He will have to "accommodate." Thus I also cannot accept the "optimists'" view of a 3 percent rate of inflation becoming more or less standard for the rest of the 1980's, a rate that would be compatible with gold at $250 an ounce. Rather I can see inflation rising above the 5 percent level—maybe even to 8 percent—sometime after mid-decade. But I cannot see it going higher before 1986. For while Volcker is still in command, at some point he will establish a limit to the amount of trade-off in terms of inflation that the Fed will accept in order to maintain recovery. Then the monetary brakes *will* be applied. Thus a revival of inflation in a couple of years, yes; runaway inflation, no. To be sure, Volcker's term runs out in 1987, and there are many indications that he will leave the job early. If he does, I would suggest you reexamine the merits of the pessimistic scenario—and its case for gold—the very day he leaves.

If not $4,400 an ounce, and if not $250, then why something in the $600 range?

A relatively moderate revival of inflation to the 5–8 percent range in 1985 under Volcker, as I am suggesting, will of itself not justify a $600-an-ounce gold price in 1987. But one must be careful not to be too logical where gold and gold prices are concerned. We are talking about a metal, the price of which is driven more by emotion than by logic. And what I expect is that when prices do start to rise, enough investors are going to say "Aha, here we go again!" to produce the result that future inflationary expectations, as unrealistic as they may be *at the time*, will drive the price of gold to levels which will be much higher than pure logic would dictate.

Therefore, on balance, I can see gold at $600 well before this decade is over.

Since I also think that the "bad-for-gold" conditions and scenario will continue through 1984 into 1985, I would not exactly rush out and load up right now (i.e., in early 1984). You can safely wait at least a year from then before considering the purchase of gold in any quantity.

However, should you sense during 1984 or early 1985 that our period of grace is going to end sooner than I currently expect—that the pessimistic scenario is about to phase in at the beginning of 1985, that Volcker is about to jump ship, and that the four key economic variables we are watching—growth, M_1, interest rates and inflation, especially inflation—are all about to go sour in a major fashion, you would be a damn fool not to go out and buy some gold right away.

How to buy it, then? There are various ways: if you want bullion, buy

Krugerrands, that South African gold coin weighing exactly one ounce. You pay a price only about 3 percent higher than the price the "big boys" pay when they buy twelve-kilo bars in Zurich, a very small premium for having the real thing in small quantities. Timothy Green, whose book *The New World of Gold* is the bible for anybody seriously interested in the subject, has pointed out that more than half of all gold taken up for investment in the last decade has been in the form of coin, and the Krugerrand has led the rest of the coins by a mile. You can buy or sell them in any major city on earth at any time.

Another sound way to "participate" in gold is through investment in South African gold-mining stocks . . . either by buying into an American mutual fund specializing in such mining stocks, such as Strategic Investments, United Services Gold Shares or Fidelity Precious Metals, or by working through a brokerage house in London which deals directly in such shares, such as Grieveson, Grant or James Cable, two of the best.

The advantage gold-mining shares *had* over bullion used to be that such stocks paid very high dividends—in the 15 percent range—and thus represented sound conservative investments purely from the income point of view. No more. In 1982–83 the prices of South African gold-mining shares went through a rise which can quite accurately be termed meteoric. Since these shares are predominantly traded in London, it is the gold-mining index of that city's *Financial Times* which provides the measure of their performance. Between the middle of 1982 and early 1983 that *F.T.* Gold-Mining Index went from 188.7 to 699.0—a rise of 270.4 percent! During that same period the Dow Jones Industrial Average went up 45 percent, and people in New York thought *that* was the bull market of the century. As gratifying as that rise in the price of gold shares must have been for people who owned them, what is disturbing about it is that during the same period the price of gold bullion went up only 65.3 percent, from $307 an ounce to $507.50. Furthermore, when the bullion price subsequently went into semicollapse, dropping $100 in one week as a result of the fall in oil prices, some of the gold shares plummeted even further—especially the marginal ones, i.e., those where production costs are so high and the grade of ore so low that at $300 the mines not only must stop paying dividends but face physical closure, while at $600 they make unexpected windfall profits, most of which they pay out in the form of dividends to speculators who have bet on their stock.

To explain these highly leveraged mines another way, at $300 their life expectancy is essentially zero—and if you just bought the shares of such a mine, that is essentially what your shares will be worth if the price stays low for very long. If, however, the price goes to $600 an ounce and stays there, that same mine will be able to stay alive, and make money, for ten more years—during which time it will be pouring out dividends, since it makes little sense for management to reinvest profits internally in what is essentially a marginal, dying enterprise. That stock, which you bought on the cheap when the gold price was only $300 an ounce, has now become a money machine. Thus, depending on current bullion prices and especially on future expectations regarding the gold price, the prices of the stocks of the marginal type of mine either zoom up dramatically or plummet. Western Areas is a typical example. During the period in question its stock went from $1.75 to $8.17 and then back down to $5.25 all in a matter of less than nine months.

What this means is that gold shares today tend to overreact on both the up-side and the down-side. When the gold-bugs are optimistic, prices are at times geared to a gold bullion price $100 to $150 an ounce higher than it actually is. When bullion collapses, the prices of gold shares tend to overshoot the other way. If you like volatility, obviously shares will be your thing, but I would rather buy gold itself.

But for those who find stocks like Western Areas too tame and really want to gamble, there are ample opportunities in the gold futures markets offered in Chicago by a division of the Chicago Mercantile Exchange, the International Monetary Market, or if you really want to go far out, through the purchase of *options* on gold *futures* at the Comex (Commodity Exchange) in New York. For $1,000 a call option allows you to buy the right, but *not the obligation,* to buy a gold futures contract at a specified price on or before a specified date. You pay a pretty hefty premium for that right, meaning that even if the gold price goes up, if it does not go up very substantially during the life of your option, you lose your thousand bucks anyway. On the other hand, you can't lose *more* than that thousand, which is what makes this sort of thing attractive to chronic losers, I guess. If, by chance, the price really takes off, you can make five or ten times what you put in.

But don't count on it. On balance you are probably better off playing options on gold futures than playing the slot machines in Vegas or Atlantic City. But only marginally so.

Which brings us back to this: if you want to buy gold, buy gold.

Chapter 16

o◯ooo◯ooo◯o

Silver

SILVER AND GOLD move together. They are both regarded as hedges against the consequences of political and economic upheaval; they are both regarded as "hard" asset hedges against inflation.

Silver, however, is much more volatile than gold. Its price went from $1.29 an ounce in the 1960's to $45 an ounce in 1980, then back down to $4.78 an ounce in 1982, back up to almost $15 in 1983, then down to $8.

The reason for this is that for the past twenty-five years there has been an added "incentive" for speculators to take a flier in silver: since 1958 they have been told that the world's silver mines are unable to produce enough silver to meet industrial demand and that, ergo, the price of silver must soon explode. Stanley Angrist, a commodity speculator who writes for *Forbes,* has said: "That one statement has probably suckered more neophyte speculators into long positions in the silver market than any other single sentence in the English language."

As we all know, this led Bunker Hunt, various Arabs, some Swiss banks and lots of suckers in the United States besides Bunker Hunt to bet their shirts on silver at various times. Almost all lost their shirts, since that yearned-for moment when the world would run out of silver never arrived.

Nor will it in the foreseeable future, since there are still *immense private hordes* of silver above ground, despite that gap between mine output and industrial consumption which has indeed existed since 1958. This horde is currently estimated at 1.37 billion ounces by one of the best-known precious metals dealers in the world, Handy & Harman. It is in the form of scrap, of melted coins, of silver stashed away in India (where it has for centuries been used to store family wealth), all of which starts to come out of the woodwork when the price gets attractive enough.

What is that price? Who knows exactly, but the best guesses of reasonable men currently put it in the $15–$20 range.

That price, therefore, probably represents the upper "logical" limit on silver in the immediate future.

I would expect silver to move in the direction of this upper limit in the years ahead. The economic reasoning behind this is precisely the same as that which prompted me to suggest that gold in the $600 range is probable by 1987: a revival of inflation and especially of exaggerated inflationary expectations.

Since I think inflation is going to remain at low levels during the next twelve months, there is hardly any reason to go out and buy silver *now*, any more than gold. But as the current recovery reaches its final stages, as the monetary authorities try to "stretch it out" with increasingly accommodating monetary policies, as labor unions start once again to overreach in their wage demands, inflation in the 5–8 percent range will return, and so will expectations that it will soon be back into double digits.

That should push gold into the $600-an-ounce range and silver to at least $15 an ounce, and probably well beyond.

If you are lucky in your timing, you might end up as one of the few who has ever made money in silver.

Chapter 17

०◯००◯००◯०

Commodities

EIGHTY-FIVE PERCENT of *all* commodity speculators get *wiped out.*
Commodity markets are the most volatile and unpredictable of any
markets on earth. To compound the problem, commodity speculation is
done on margin, which means that often with a $5,000 "investment" you
can control $100,000 of assets. What this also means is that even though
you might be right in the long run in regard to the trend in the price of
cocoa, or sugar, or pork bellies, or in the level of interest rates or the stock
market averages, a temporary "aberration" in this trend of, say, 4 percent
in the *other* direction will threaten your entire "investment." You will
then get a margin call from your broker demanding that either you put
up some more cash or be sold out. In the end you send more cash, and
you still get sold out . . . at least 85 percent of the time.

Lesson: don't fool around with commodities.

Chapter 18

oᏇoooᏇoooᏇo

Real Estate

REAL ESTATE has been by far the investment that has produced the
greatest profits for the greatest numbers of Americans during the past
decade, the result of the most dramatic run-up in real estate prices in our
history. Between 1975 and 1980 it was usual to see the price of houses
in certain parts of the country rising at rates of 20–25 percent a year, year
after year.

One reason for such spectacular performance was that housing started
from a very low initial price base, largely because of its abundance, an
abundance which resulted from the fact that it has always been remarkably cheap and easy for almost anybody in America to *finance* the purchase of a house. There are three reasons for this:

First, for years Regulation Q put a ceiling of 5.5 percent on the interest
rate that savings and loans could pay on savings deposits. Since that was
0.25 percent higher than the banks could legally pay, the S&Ls accumulated huge amounts of very *low-cost* capital which they were then
able to devote to mortgages at extraordinarily low *fixed* interest rates—
7 or 8 percent for thirty years—and still make good profits.

Second, the *real* cost of that 7 or 8 percent was cut by a quarter or a
third or even a half because our government, unlike most others, subsi-
dizes housing for everybody, including even the richest, by allowing its
citizens to deduct interest costs from their taxable income.

Third, if America had one resource that was abundant almost everywhere, it was land. As a result of Eisenhower's highway construction
program, which made Hitler's *Autobahnen* look like a pilot project, the
United States built a transportation system which turned millions of

America's inexpensive rural acres into suburban housing developments.

Before the early or mid-1970's housing was so abundant in the United States that nobody ever really thought of it as anything but shelter. You bought a house to *live in,* not to *make money on.* Only then did it occur to us that inflation had changed things. The prices of *real* assets had come to life—first silver, then diamonds, then gold, and finally what I like to call "American gold," real estate.

Housing prices skyrocketed. But then in 1981–82 down came the sledgehammer of Reagan's deep recession, which not only reduced the rate of inflation but for a while actually eliminated it; for months it was down to absolute zero. With price rises temporarily a thing of the past, the need for hedges against inflation also temporarily disappeared. The result was a dramatic plunge in the prices of "hard" asset investments. Silver went from $45 an ounce down to the $5–$10 range, gold from its historic high of $850 an ounce down to the $400 range, diamonds from $60,000 a carat for the D-flawless gem down to $14,000.

While that slaughter was going on, investors in the ultimate hard asset, real estate, were shaken. Some marginal speculators even went to the wall and saw their properties foreclosed. But in general the price reaction from the historic highs was relatively mild. The national average price of a new one-family house went from the all-time peak of around $100,000 to the $87,000 range in the first half of 1983. Such "performance" in the face of disinflation points out a basic difference between real estate and almost all other types of "hard" asset investments: people need houses—to live in—regardless of the prevailing rates of inflation or interest. One can hardly say that an equal need exists for silver futures, Krugerrands or such collectibles as comic books and old cars.

Since the demand for houses-to-live-in is constant over and above the on-again, off-again demand for houses-as-investments, real estate is probably the soundest, most reliable, least volatile "hedge" against inflation. It does *not* necessarily collapse when prices in general stop moving up.

At the same time it should be quite obvious that real estate is still a lousy investment when inflation is 3 percent and mortgages are at 13–14 percent, as they are at the moment I write. Don't look for solace in the fact that you are in the 50 percent tax bracket and the 13 percent you are paying to the bank each year is really only 6.5 percent since Uncle Sam chips in for the other half. In 1983 you were still losing money on your investment in real estate, instead of making maybe 20 percent in the stock market, or enjoying a 12 percent yield from your bonds, or getting "just" 8 percent a year from your money market fund or account.

Real estate is hard to sell in bad times, as millions of people have found out lately. Aside from this liquidity factor comes the added shock sellers face when they find out that list price is by no means equal to the cash price you can realistically get when the real estate market turns sour.

The question now is this: How long will these "bad times" last? "Bad times" for real estate have their own special definition. The key "swing" factor is the "real" interest rate—the difference between the rate of inflation and the mortgage rate. When these rates are grossly positive, i.e., when mortgage interest rates are 13 percent and inflation is 3 percent, meaning the real positive interest rate is 10 percent, and when it appears as if this situation could last for years, real estate is a terrible investment. That's right now.

"Good times" return for real estate if and when real interest rates turn negative, for instance if mortgage rates come down to 10 percent and stay there for a while, and inflation starts to head up, and eventually goes to, say, 14 percent—meaning that real interest rates would move from +10 percent to −4 percent—then, and probably only then, does real estate, at least in the form of one-family dwellings, once again become an excellent speculation.

The trick is to catch mortgage rates while they are "low" relative to the next prospective "high" in the rate of inflation.

What then is going to be the "low" in mortgage rates in the foreseeable future? And what is going to be the prospective "high" in the rate of inflation? What are going to be the prospective *real* interest rates that will result? And how will all this translate into average increases in housing prices during the next three or four years?

You might say that anybody would be very foolish to attempt to answer these questions. But the whole idea of this book is to take a stab at precisely such things. So . . .

Mortgage rates: we will probably not see fixed mortgage interest rates fall below 10 percent in this decade. Period. The *cost* of money that faces mortgage lenders in the foreseeable future, as they compete with the U.S. government, corporate America and myriad other financial institutions for money in a now unregulated market, simply will not allow them to *lend* it out at anything below 10 percent and still make a profit. Thus any rate that you can lock in at or near that number is going to be your "low" where mortgage costs are concerned.

Inflation rates: Ah, if one only knew for sure, even for half-sure. My guess is that in 1984 they are going to stay relatively low by standards of the recent past, i.e., in the 4 percent range. But I also have the feeling that they *may* be heading up after mid-decade. How high? To the 5–8 percent range would be my guess. Pressure from constant "excessive" increases in money supply evoked by the necessity to finance continuing very high deficits will push the rate of inflation up, but downward pressure, exerted by continuing slack in the real economy—unemployment, underutilization of plant and equipment capacity—and foreign competition will ensure that it does not become excessive . . . *in the short run.*

Your guess may well be different and in the end better. For instance, if you subscribe to my pessimistic scenario, you will be planning for a major acceleration in the rate of inflation after mid-decade, well into double digits, to be followed, with a lag, by major increases in nominal interest rates. That would mean that a new "window of opportunity" to make money in all types of real estate has already begun to open up, since conditions in a year or two will very closely resemble those which prevailed during the post-1975 period. If you wholly subscribe to this pessimistic scenario, the best thing you could do is lock in a 12 percent mortgage right now, since the rate of inflation will soon overtake it, and you will make a pile.

However, if you accept the optimistic scenario in its entirety, you are anticipating that during the rest of this decade inflation will remain around 4 percent. Nominal interest rates will gradually decline into single digits, even long-term rates, but they will stay above the rate of inflation. If *either* the totally optimistic scenario *or* my more moderate middle-of-the-road one proves correct, real estate investment will not be profitable . . . and that because of real interest rates. If I am right about inflation increasing moderately after mid-decade to the 5–8 percent range, and if I am also right that mortgage rates are hardly going to fall below 10 percent, you could *at best* "lock in" a mortgage interest rate that would *exceed* the general rate of inflation in a couple of years by 2 percent, the real rate of interest. If the optimistic scenario proves to be the right one, you would probably also end up facing a positive real interest rate in this same 2–3 percent range, should inflation settle in at 3–4 percent per annum and interest rates come down to 6 percent or 7 percent. In both cases you would be continually paying more to carry the house you invested in than its market value would be appreciating in the pull of inflation. In both cases you would not make any money in real terms if the object of your investment/speculation was a single-family dwelling.

Let's pursue this further and take a house that you purchase today for $125,000. You pay 20 percent, or $25,000, down. The rest you finance for thirty years at 12 percent per annum. The "carrying" charges on that investment are going to be $1,028.63 a month for principal and interest, which when annualized and combined with other basic charges gives the following picture:

Principal and interest	$12,343.56
Real estate taxes (San Francisco)	1,462.50
Insurance	500.00
Total	$14,306.06

If the rate of inflation is in the 5–6 percent range, your new house will probably increase in value at the same rate, or by $6,250. This is by no means sure, however, and I will explain why in a moment. In gross terms you would lose $14,306.06 in costs less $6,250 in appreciation in the value of your house, which equals $8,056.06. Even when you take into account the deduction of interest costs and real estate taxes from your taxable income, you would still lose money on such an investment. If you are in the 40 percent bracket your absolute loss would be in the range of $2,500. And don't forget that you are also forfeiting income on the money you used for the down payment—money that could be earning you 8 or 10 percent had you invested it elsewhere.

Let's "improve" conditions (from the speculator's standpoint) and say that in 1985, even if the rate of inflation continues to be moderate, housing prices will start to "outperform" inflation by, say, 3 percent (due to a growing shortage of new housing units) with the result that prices will be going up at a rate of 9 percent per annum. Under such conditions and assumptions, in 1985 the value of your house would increase by $10,500. If you are in the 40 percent tax bracket and take advantage of the interest and real estate tax deductions, you would be ahead exactly $1,700 in 1985, a return of 7 percent on your invested capital of $25,000, although thus far the cumulative two-year result would still leave you $800 in the hole. Your $25,000 equity investment would be worth only $24,200 after two years.

You would have done considerably better by simply putting your down payment of $25,000 in a money market account at the bank. It would probably be worth at least $29,000, since the interest rate the banks pay on such accounts is essentially "indexed" to the rate of inflation, and would have been rising just as inflation was rising and the price of houses was rising. Except that it would have been a lot less risky.

Aha, you are thinking, but who says that the price of houses is not going to increase a *lot* faster than the future rate of inflation?

I do, and here's why: houses in the United States, which seemed so *underpriced* at the beginning of the 1970's, have risen in price so far and so fast that they are now *overpriced* relative to the income qualifications of 90 percent of American families. Sometimes we forget exactly what has happened to housing costs. According to the National Association of Realtors, the *median* price of an existing detached house in the United States in 1970 was $23,000 nationally; in 1983 it was $68,300. In the western part of the United States the median price went from $24,300 in 1970 to $92,300 in 1983. The national *average* (not median) price of a *new* home, which is calculated by the *Wall Street Journal* every week, is in this same $90,000–$100,000 range. No matter how they are measured, prices have more than *tripled* during the past decade.

Incomes, however, did not triple, by a long shot. In 1973 median family income was $12,000; in 1983 it was $24,000. Banks and savings and loans use the rule of thumb that 25 percent, maximum, of your family's gross income should go to housing—i.e., into paying principal, interest, taxes and insurance. In the early 1970's this meant that 44 percent of American families qualified for that median-priced $23,000 home (remember: mortgage rates *then* were 7–8 percent); today (with mortgage rates in the 13 + percent range) just 10 percent—*ten percent of all American families* —can "qualify" to buy an existing *median-*priced American home, to say nothing of that *average-*priced *new* home which costs almost $100,000.

In other words, we now face a tremendous "affordability" gap. Americans all have the same *desire* to purchase a home in 1983 as they had in 1971, but now only one family in ten is able to.

This sudden inability of buyers to finance the purchase of single-family dwellings has been matched by a sudden growth in the number of sellers, or at least of *latent* sellers. For there are now an awful lot of people in the United States—people who are getting older, their children gone, their income prospects no longer so good—who want to "cash in" on their now very expensive dwellings. In the early 1980's when mortgage rates were 15 or 17 percent and the activity in the real estate market was dormant, they really had no choice but to wait until conditions got better. Conditions now *are* better, but they will never return to what these people were used to because *in the future money is always going to cost more than it did in the past.* It is this structural upward shift in the cost of financing which is as responsible for the drastically changed outlook for housing as the tripling in price of the house itself.

For the banks and S&L's no longer have any *free* money: even on checking accounts of the NOW or Super-NOW type they must pay interest. Nor do they any longer even have lots of *cheap* money since

Regulation Q was abolished. They must go out and *buy* almost every nickel they get. This puts a permanent *floor* on their lending rates. They can hardly pay you 8 percent on your money market account and then lend you that same money for 7.5 percent for thirty years on a house, as they did for Grandma. Thus, with prices more than triple what they were, and with interest costs almost double, who can afford a typical American single-family dwelling? Answer: very few Americans.

To be sure, *should* the optimistic scenario work out in spades; *should* real economic growth in America now shift upward to a 5 percent average annual rate for an extended period of time; *should* this be accompanied by a more or less permanent 3 percent rate of inflation, and 6–7 percent interest rates—then the affordability gap would certainly narrow, since incomes would be rising twice as fast as the cost of houses, while financing costs would be sinking. But whether houses would be a good *investment* even then remains highly questionable. For this would essentially mean a return to the conditions of the 1950's—the Eisenhower years. As far as I can recall, nobody exactly got rich speculating in houses then.

But I consider this extremely optimistic scenario just as unlikely as the extremely pessimistic one. The middle-of-the-road scenario which I endorse would leave the current affordability gap more or less intact.

Under such conditions, what are people who need housing to live in going to do? Increasingly they are going to have no choice but to rent. The result is going to be a gradual "Europeanization" of housing in the United States. Many of our sons and daughters, not to speak of *their* sons and daughters, are going to live in rented apartments rather than in houses of their own.

As a result fewer housing units will be built in the 1980's compared to the numbers produced in the 1970's and 1960's. Developers will continue to be very reluctant to go way out on a limb hoping for mass sales of $110,000 houses, while banks are going to continue to be very wary of financing any such development projects for exactly the same reason.

The net result is probably going to be this:

a. As population grows and shifts from low-growth to high-growth areas of the country, the "stock" of housing is going to start to run short in various regions of the United States.

b. Because of the "affordability" gap, more and more people are going to be trying to rent units of that now increasingly scarce housing stock.

c. Therefore the *immediate* shortage will be in rental units, not in single-family dwellings, with the result that rents will go up, and rapidly —*regardless of the rate of inflation.*

Conclusion: investing in multiple-family rental units probably makes sense. The "best-to-be-hoped-for" situation is likely one in which you could count on steadily rising rental rates (except in areas where rent controls exist . . . areas that investors should avoid like the plague) and *steady* interest costs in the 10 to 12 percent range, which is by no means impossible under reasonably optimistic economic assumptions concerning the future. But even if conditions are somewhat less than ideal, you should remember that since 1981 real estate for investment purposes has been made dramatically more attractive by the Economic Recovery Tax Act, especially with respect to how this legislation affects depreciation allowances.

Depreciation: that is yet another financial term that causes eyes to cross. But it is important, believe me, and it can all be explained in two paragraphs. Maybe three.

Depreciation is a tax deduction—a *mandatory* tax deduction—designed to reflect the loss in value that a building undergoes as it gets older. It used to be that you could amortize a building only over thirty years— or, in plain English, that you could deduct one thirtieth of the building's original cost from your taxable income each year for thirty years. The 1981 Economic Recovery Tax Act cut that period in half—to fifteen years. Not only that, but it also allows for a 175 percent acceleration of depreciation within that fifteen years, meaning that the first year you can deduct not just one fifteenth of the building's value from your taxable income, but almost double that amount.

Let's go back to that $125,000 house to see what a difference this makes. Remember, we concluded that if you bought that home to live in but also in the hope that you would make a nice profit on it, you were making a mistake. You would lose money, at least during the first few years. Let's take that same house, but this time assume that you are buying it purely for investment purposes, that you plan to rent it out indefinitely. Assuming that $100,000 of that price was for the building (and the rest for the land, which is not depreciable), and further assuming you are in the 40 percent tax bracket, the cost/benefit calculation would now look like this:

COSTS:

Principal and interest	$ 12,343.56
Real estate taxes	1,462.50
Insurance	500.00
Total	$ 14,306.06
	the first year

BENEFITS:

5 percent appreciation in value of property	$ 6,250.00
Tax benefit of deduction of interest	4,800.00
Tax benefit of deduction of taxes	584.80
Tax benefit of accelerated depreciation	12,000.00
Total appreciation + tax savings	$ 23,634.80
	the first year

Now, before you start jumping up and down and start recalculating last year's taxes, wait for the restrictions on these depreciation windfalls:

1. They do *not* apply to properties bought before 1981.

2. They do *not* apply to the home you live in.

3. They do *not* apply to a second (vacation) home if you occupy it yourself for more than 10 percent of the time.

4. They do *not* apply to land.

These benefits are restricted to buildings, structures and even personal property bought and held for *investment*, for example investment in rental units. Whereas *without* the benefit of depreciation you would have lost over $2,500 on our "model" real estate purchase the first year, *with* the tax benefits of accelerated depreciation you would now be ahead by $9,328.74. That is why some people call Mr. Reagan the rich man's President. If you want to study how you can best combine real estate with tax advantages as an *individual* investor, i.e., doing it on your own, the best book I have yet seen on this subject is *The Smart Investor's Guide to Real Estate*, written by Robert Bruss, who also writes the nationally syndicated newspaper column "Real Estate Mailbag."

Where will the best regions for such investments be? MIT's Lester Thurow, the inventor of the concept of the zero-sum society, has indirectly provided us with the answer. Even if you think the growth prospects for the country as a whole are not nearly as hot as the optimists would have us believe, and that we face a period of extended economic stagnation during much of the remainder of this decade, this does not mean that while the nation stands relatively still and Michigan actually declines in terms of both business activity and working population, California cannot be gaining in both respects at the same time. Even though the economic pie stays the same size, slice A can continue to grow in a zero-sum society, although this means that slice B will be shrinking. Obviously you will want to direct your real estate investment dollars at the "A's" of this country.

The "A's" will be first and foremost those areas with a high concentration of high-tech industries, meaning primarily California and parts of Massachusetts and Texas . . . though not the energy centers there. The growth of these industries will have a very substantial local ripple effect on the surrounding "support" industries. Housing and real estate in general will be among the primary beneficiaries of this process. The reverse will be true of those "B" areas with high concentrations of basic industries —areas in the so-called heartland of America. A recent study by the Congressional Budget Office estimates that between now and 1990 automation and capacity cutbacks in basic industry will eliminate three million manufacturing jobs, and that by the year 2000, factory robots will be doing what seven million human beings are doing right now in Pennsylvania, Ohio, Michigan and parts of adjacent states such as New York and New Jersey and Kentucky. That is going to mean an awful lot of empty houses in the upper Midwest and Northeast as a result of the exodus of population to those areas that *make* those robots.

But the stimulus does not necessarily have to be high-tech. Florida will continue to see a steady inflow of senior citizens from the North and immigrants from the Caribbean attracted by the increasing Latinization of south Florida. Here the stimulus to real estate will come from a combination of above-average population growth and the rise of Miami as a vibrant commercial and financial center. Virginia real estate cannot help but be strong since it is next door to one of the biggest growth sectors of all, one that keeps growing no matter what, namely the public sector in Washington, D.C.

But remember that unexpected events can turn today's winners suddenly into losers. Which brings us back yet again to our old friend, the oil price. In the 1970's some of the most attractive areas for real estate investments in the United States were Denver, Houston and Dallas because the growth industry of the 1970's, at least in terms of the money it was throwing off to those on the *producing* end, was energy, especially oil and gas. What was good for real estate in Riyadh was almost as good for real estate in Oklahoma City. In Dallas and Denver, as in Mexico City, everybody thought that since the price of oil was inevitably going from

$40 to $60 to $100 a barrel, real estate in the energy centers would be good until the end of this century and probably beyond. Now, as a result of the retreat in energy prices, the outlook for energy centers has drastically changed, if not from boom to bust, at least from boom to relatively slow times. As goes oil, so also goes real estate in these places. With the outlook for oil what it is, real estate in the energy centers of Texas might be a good thing to avoid at this time.

So much for the "why" and the "where," but what about the "how"? As with stocks and bonds, I think that where real estate is concerned, the best approach is to rely upon the experts. And the best vehicles offering the expert help you most probably need are the limited partnerships that have grown up all over the United States designed specifically to provide *managed* tax-sheltered investments in real estate.

Such limited partnerships, which are really nothing more than real estate mutual funds of a sort, come in all colors, shapes and sizes. If you want to know all about them, there are dozens of books on the subject, but probably the most helpful is *Shelter What You Make—Minimize the Take,* written by one of this country's foremost financial planners, Beverly Tanner. The principle is always the same, however. A general partner (the expert) puts together real estate deals, and you get a piece of his deals and share in all the tax and depreciation benefits *now,* plus the final capital gain (you hope) seven or ten years *from now,* when "your" joint property is sold at that immense profit. In the meantime you have the pleasure of being an absentee landlord, leaving all the details to the experts. Even the big financial conglomerates like Merrill Lynch and American Express now package these types of investments, and some have the added advantage of allowing you to bail out before "maturity." It used to be with all such partnerships, and still is with most, that you were irrevocably locked in for many years. No more. Penn Mutual Life Insurance, for example, through a subsidiary, gives investors in its limited partnership an annual option of cashing out after only four years. The ultimate specialists in this field, such as Consolidated Capital of Emeryville, California, or Landsing of Palo Alto, keep coming up with ever more innovative packages, such as programs that match up a group of tax-exempt investors who want income and appreciation (such as pension funds) with groups of individuals in the 50 percent tax bracket who want big write-offs in an effort to squeeze out the very last penny of profit for all.

How much can you reasonably expect to make on such investments— meaning your total after-tax return? Probably at least as much as you would make with a municipal bond fund—9 percent, say. The difference is that you have a much greater potential for a substantial capital gain in real estate than you ever will have in municipal bonds. The best thing if you are in a high tax bracket is to get some of both. The Economic Recovery Tax Act means that Uncle Sam is now a major partner in real estate investments, just as he has always been in municipal bonds. This is one big reason why the rich will continue to get richer.

One last warning, however. *Because* the Economic Recovery Tax Act, which cut the depreciation rate on housing units to fifteen years, makes this type of investment so attractive to the rich, *billions* of dollars are now pouring into real estate syndications. If this price continues long enough, a rental property glut will develop not only in Dallas and Denver but all over the United States, and these deals will *all* begin to turn sour.

On the other hand, *because* the rich are on to a good thing, which is why those billions are pouring in, it seems probable that Congress will change the law, raising the depreciation period back to twenty-five or even thirty years, eliminating this tax "loophole" and putting an end to this investment game. If this occurs fairly soon—and I believe it will—no rental property glut will develop.

Therefore move now, before Congress does.

Chapter 19

o◯ooo◯ooo◯o

Tax Shelters

Except for real estate and municipal bonds, I would avoid being talked into investing in any other types of fancy tax shelters, be they oil and gas ventures, R&D schemes or race horses. Too often you end up "saving" taxes but also losing all your money. Now that the top tax rate has been reduced to 50 percent, who needs such grief?

But there are two tax shelters that everyone, and I mean *everyone*, should use: the Individual Retirement Accounts, which all of us are eligible for now, and the Keogh plans for the self-employed. The amounts annually invested in these vehicles can be deducted from your taxable income, and the income that these accounts then generate is not taxable until you start taking it out in your retirement years, when you will probably be in a much lower tax bracket.

Where to invest the $2,000 a year you can put into the IRAs, or the up to $30,000 in Keoghs? I would suggest you look at both high-income-producing investments and situations that promise high growth potential in the longer run. The idea, of course, is to be in things that would cost you a lot of taxes were you to invest in them—successfully, one hopes—directly. If you share my moderately optimistic view of our short-run economic future, ideally right now you would have some money in a bond fund. By this I do *not* mean a municipal bond fund, of course, since income from them is tax-free anyway. Nor would I suggest a fund investing exclusively in government notes and bonds, since the yields they offer are too low. Go for funds that invest in high-quality corporate bonds: they offer the best combination of high interest yield, relative safety and liquidity.

But the majority of IRA/Keogh funds should probably be in stocks—invested partially in an aggressive "growth" fund and partially in a fund specializing in high-tech stocks. Don't worry about periodic gyrations in the performance of these funds. Since your money is essentially locked into IRAs and Keoghs for the long run anyway, what you are looking for is a bonanza in capital gains seven or ten years from now.

Chapter 20

∘◯∘∘◯∘∘◯∘

Stocks

IT USED TO BE that when you thought about "investment" you automatically thought about the stock market. The alternative to "the market" was, in essence, just plain savings—i.e., a bank account paying 5.25 percent.

No longer. The revolution in investment thinking really began with the breakup of the banks' monopoly on savings brought on by the advent of the money market funds in the 1970's. Millions of people, perhaps unconsciously, made the first real investment decision of their lives when they pulled their money out of the bank and gave it to a money fund manager who paid them *dividends* on their *investment* instead of *interest* on their *savings.* Feet wet, when the new money market accounts at the banks offered a better deal, these same people moved for the second time. What I am suggesting is that in the 1980's we now have an immensely larger pool of demonstrably *mobile* funds looking for a better way to make money with money.

On the other side, we also have a vastly larger array of investment vehicles, accessible to millions of people with only a few thousand dollars to invest. We have tax-free municipal bond funds which today, as we have seen, yield the taxable equivalent of 15–20 percent to people in higher income tax brackets; we have gold, which since 1975 has been legal for Americans to invest in for the first time in most of their lives; even the Treasury is promoting its bills and notes and bonds and vying for these dollars. So it's no longer true that "investment" means "stocks." Stocks now have to compete for investment dollars; to compete they must outperform some or all of the above alternative investments listed, or at least hold out the reasonable *promise* of such outperformance, one that will compensate the investor for the risk that everybody knows is inherent in the notoriously volatile and generally unpredictable stock markets.

Before the summer of 1982 the market had failed to perform for more than a decade. For thirteen long years between 1969 and 1982 the Dow meandered between 500 and 1,000, never breaking into new territory. Then in 1983 the market finally moved decisively and massively into the 1,000–1,500 range. Why did it take so long? The answer, to simplify matters greatly, is that for a very long time we simply had too much inflation and too little growth. The multiple that investors in the stock market were willing to put on the average company's earnings was only seven times. By contrast, in 1971 and 1972, when inflation was around 2 percent and the economy was growing nicely, and interest rates were 4.5 percent, the market was willing to pay multiples of eighteen to one.

By 1983 we had returned to 1971–72 conditions in the overall economy, as both the inflation rate and the real growth rate were in the 3–5 percent range and short-term interest rates, while not at 4.5 percent, were at least almost back into single digits. Provided these conditions last for a while, and I think they will, I would not be surprised to see multiples return, if not to the level of eighteen, then at least to the levels of thirteen to fifteen. Propelled by the current recovery and with earnings recovering rapidly, a Dow moving in the 1,100 to 1,600 range between now and mid-1985 is a distinct possibility.

Therefore, I think that *into 1985* stocks will continue to be a good investment. This conclusion will hold whether you accept the optimistic or pessimistic overall economic scenario for the *longer* run, i.e., after 1985. Should a low-inflationary recovery continue *beyond* 1985, then I would guess that the general uptrend in the stock market would do likewise. But as much as I would like to believe that, I don't. *My* scenario is the following: after mid-decade this recovery will be in its third year, and history tells us that at that stage bottlenecks and labor shortages inevitably begin to develop in various key sectors of the economy. Costs and prices will be driven up. When the monetary brakes are applied in an attempt to counter such developments, interest rates will rise. The recovery will begin to end, and those preconditions for a booming stock market—high growth and low rates of inflation and interest—will begin to disappear.

My scenario is based upon the belief that the business cycle is *not* dead, that it is inherent in our capitalistic system. Thus those who think that the current upward movement will continue forever, as investors did in the 1960's who thought that the business cycle had been "fine-tuned" out of existence, will be disappointed. So I do not see the Dow at 3,000, as so many who have recently turned from utter pessimism to total optimism would have us believe. *Half* the level is, after all, not that bad, is it?

So: the stock market, yes, at least for the medium term. But what stocks in that stock market? Again a simple answer: invest in the stocks of those industry groups which promise the most growth, those which will probably continue to grow even if the general economy once again turns sour, even if only temporarily, after mid-decade. For when I talk about investing in the stocks of companies in such industry groups, I mean making a five-year commitment: buy 'em and lock 'em up. Since such groups tend to behave in a more volatile fashion than most other stock groups, this "lock up" principle is especially important. Unless you make a longer-term commitment, there is a real danger that you will be "psyched out" by short-term price oscillations, which can lead to panic selling followed by panic buying, and result in your suffering a bad case of costly financial whiplash.

But does this approach really make sense if the pessimistic scenario prevails in 1985 and thereafter? If we sink back into stagflation, won't everybody's future be cut short?

By no means. And we return again to the man who has explained this best, Lester Thurow, and his concept of a zero-sum society. In a society where the overall pie is no longer growing, *some* slices of that pie *will* nevertheless continue to grow—at the expense of other slices. Thus, according to Thurow, the overall economy of the United States could stagnate while California continues to grow, as Michigan and Ohio shrink. One of the reasons California will grow is that it is there that many of the companies which make up the "sunrise" industries are concentrated, the comers, while the upper Midwest is where the "sunset" industries are situated, industries which have reached maturity and are now in the gradual, irrevocable process of decline.

Since, as we have already noted, those sunset industries are finished as the providers of growth, the creators of wealth, for American society, why invest in them for the *longer* term? They have no future in which to invest. To be sure, there will always be Chryslers that confound the experts by rising from their deathbeds. Those who gambled and bought the stock in 1981 made a lot of money. But do you *really* believe that Chrysler is still going to be around at the end of this decade? I doubt it, therefore I would not invest in it.

But what "sunrise" industries should you buy? Answer: those involved in high technology, at least high technology of the type where the United

States is *globally dominant* now and promises to remain so during our generation. That narrows it down very significantly, for it means predominantly electronics as applied to the fields of data-processing, instrumentation, communications, aerospace and defense systems.

Narrowing it down still further, it means IBM (whose area of *global* dominance is and will be large main-frame computers), but it also means medium-sized companies like NBI and Intecom, which are in the process of building their own globally dominant positions in their specialized fields of office automation. In instrumentation it means one company, Hewlett-Packard, which not only leads the world in this field but is also generally regarded as one of the three best managed corporations in the United States.

Two more areas in which the United States has absolute unchallenged world dominance are *aerospace,* with General Dynamics and Boeing in a truly incomparable global position of leadership, and *defense electronics,* where nobody can begin to challenge Hughes, Sanders and Loral.

In *communications* AT&T is so obvious that we tend to overlook it, but there are a few other companies, infinitesimal by comparison, which have picked off segments of the communications industry and developed global technological leadership within them, such as Rolm where the PBX business is concerned, and Northern Telecom, which leads the way in land-based communications technology from its home in Canada. Motorola has a lock on cellular mobile radio technology. Satellite communications is an absolute American "province," with Hughes supplying the equipment and Comsat putting it into place and managing it for the world.

Where American leadership is being seriously challenged, however, is in components, the development of integrated circuits with a huge storage capacity—256,000 bits of information on one chip, as compared to the most advanced chip available up to now, the 64K, with a storage capacity of "only" 64,000 bits. The challenge is more than just one for the market, for whoever wins this race can claim global technological leadership where these basic building blocks for the electronics industry are concerned. If the Japanese win, can a major Japanese challenge for global leadership in the equipment industry be far off? Will Fujitsu become the IBM of the 1990's? If so, maybe one should be "locking up" *Japanese* electronics stocks, not American.

I have spent a fair amount of my life in Silicon Valley in California, while I was with the Stanford Research Institute doing multiclient research studies aimed at providing a framework for long-range planning by the largest companies in this field—American, British, Dutch, Japanese. Later I was active in investment banking, providing emerging electronics companies with seed capital and then advising them and/or sitting on their boards, companies located in a dozen different countries, including the United States, Germany, the United Kingdom, Italy, Belgium, Holland and Austria. What struck home time and time again was this: the American electronics industry has both a dynamic and a resilience unparalleled in the world today. So while it now seems sure that the Japanese will be first to come to market with that 256K RAM (random access memory), the Americans are probably still going to reap most of the harvest. The Japanese may initially dominate the "merchant" or open market for chips that are not built to meet any specific design applications and are sold in bulk. But the American semiconductor producers will ultimately dominate the much more important "captive" market, which is composed of the largest users of such chips. For what we are—finally —seeing in the United States is a movement toward an integration of equipment and components producers. Thus IBM, the biggest equipment producer of all, recently made a massive investment in Intel, one of America's leading manufacturers of components. This was contrary to all previous IBM policy. What it means is that when Intel's 256K RAMs are ready to go, IBM—the world's largest user of components—will no doubt use them and not their Japanese equivalents. With their financial and research resources now combined, IBM/Intel are going to be very hard to beat. Motorola, the experts say, is probably in the best position to challenge Intel. However, right behind *them* are several smaller, American innovators—like LSI Logic or VLSI Technology—which are fooling around with radically new techniques for producing such memory devices that, if successful, could put this segment of the American electronics industry back into a position of global dominance across a broad spectrum.

Genetic engineering is the other industry in which America has taken a quantum leap forward relative to the rest of the world. The first and most sensational applications of this technology have involved gene-splicing in the pharmaceutical field, enabling man to "mass-produce" interferon for the treatment of certain types of cancer. Such California companies as Genentech and Cetus have led the way. But it has now become clear that as genetic engineering is applied to one facet of human activity after another, this technology may well become to our society in the year 2,000 what electronics is to us today.

Recently one of the men who run Hewlett-Packard told me that when his electronics engineers get too cocky he reminds them that in ten years genetic engineering may make them obsolete. Interestingly, a couple of weeks later it was announced that Hewlett-Packard and Genentech had gotten together in a joint venture to develop and produce equipment designed to increasingly automate the gene-splicing process—so-called "gene machines"—which should increase productivity in this new industry a hundred-, even a thousand-fold, and make possible drastic cost reductions. Until that happens, the best course to follow in regard to investing in genetic engineering companies is probably still to "look but don't touch."

Enough. What I am suggesting is that when you invest in the stock market, you take risk. When you take risk, you might as well have the *promise* that the reward you will eventually get is immense. In my judgment, investment in high-tech fields in the United States holds just such promise. To be sure, risk-taking can also go *too* far. Thus you may have noticed that almost none of the high-tech stocks I have mentioned thus far are "hot new issues." Rather, they are stocks of already large companies, companies that are here for keeps, companies that have the resources to *stay* on the leading edge of these new technologies and probably *continue* to dominate their markets. One example: IBM, a late starter in the personal computer field, is now expected to get 40 percent of that market within the next two years. Thus I would suggest that at least half your high-tech stock portfolio be composed of these types of stocks. Go for broke with the other half, in the hope that one or two of the hot new issues you acquire turn out to be an Apple or a Genentech, and more than compensate for the stocks of those promising small companies that never made it into the big leagues.

The other way, not necessarily an alternative but rather a complementary approach to investments in stocks, is to play the cycles. Wait for the right conditions for an upward movement in the market to develop— falling inflation, rising real growth—and then play the market in general. When the cycle appears to be ending—inflation rising, growth stalling— get out. Remember Samuelson.

How to do it?

The best way to approach the stock market, in my judgment, is to recognize your amateur status in such matters from the very outset, and search out the best professional you can find to run your money for you in the way you want your money run.

So how do you find a money manager whom you can trust?

First and foremost: check track records. Let's first look at my Plan A for approaching the stock market—buying stocks of emerging high-tech

companies and locking them up for five years. Some of the most know-
ledgeable people in the world where investment in high-technology stocks
is concerned are at Hambrecht & Quist, the San Francisco investment
banking firm that provides capital to emerging Silicon Valley firms and
then brings their shares to the public if things work out. Apple Computer
and Genentech are among their "babies." They have put together an
index tracing the development of the prices of the stocks in which they
are interested, shown in Figure 22.

FIGURE 22

Hambrecht & Quist Technology Stock Index Versus Standard & Poor's and the
Dow Jones Industrial Average

FOR THE PURPOSE OF COMPARISON ALL INDEXES HAVE BEEN SET AT 100 AT DECEMBER 31, 1973

Not bad: an annual average of 29 percent increase over almost a decade.
To be sure, it has been anything but a one-way street. Such high-tech
stocks have a high "beta factor," technical jargon that means that their
historic behavior indicates that they tend to rise twice as high and fall
twice as far as the stock market as a whole. Thus, when the market as a
whole stalled in the second half of 1983, the Hambrecht & Quist family
of stocks plunged in price. But who cares—if they are bought as a "lock-

up"? The problem with Hambrecht & Quist is that although they will manage your money, you have to have $5 *million* before they *really* become interested in doing so. So scratch that.

But there are others in the field that, like Hambrecht & Quist, specialize in financing high-technology companies and, once they are going strong, sell their stocks to the public. If you are a regular client, you will get an allocation of such stocks at their new-issue price and over time can build up a portfolio, which you can balance by simultaneously building up equity positions in the IBMs and Hewlett-Packards. Two such investment banking firms are in San Francisco: Robertson, Colman & Stephens, and Montgomery Securities. Two on the East Coast of similarly very high stature are L. F. Rothschild, Unterberg, Towbin in New York and Alex. Brown & Sons in Baltimore.

If you use this approach, my advice is to stick to such quality underwriters. They screen out the marginal firms very early and very quickly, the ones that then go to equally marginal underwriters who flog their stocks to the public and then walk away when the companies go under, as a high percentage of such companies inevitably do.

For those of you who don't have the capital to get one of these investment houses to "accept" you as a client, there are now dozens of mutual funds that specialize in high-tech stocks. But there are only two that have been doing this for years, and which have good track records that can be checked: the Nautilus Fund and the Explorer Fund. Of the newer ones, Alliance Technology Fund and the Fidelity Group's high-tech fund have management that is generally regarded as superior by the high-technology investment community.

If you want to do it yourself, an excellent book tells you enough to get started: *High Tech: How to Find and Profit from Today's New Super Stocks* by Albert Toney and Thomas Tilling. But although I like the book, I definitely do *not* advise taking this approach. Amateurs playing a professional's game end up losers.

How to implement Plan B—playing the market as a whole when the time looks right? Traditionally the way to do this was to just turn over your money to the trust department of an American bank and let it do its thing. The problem today is that most American banks will not even consider taking on the management of an investment portfolio unless the amount involved is at least $500,000. So that leaves most of us out, doesn't it? Many people who have left their money to trust departments in past years would say: "Be happy they *won't* take your money." For during the past thirty years it was not at all unusual for banks to rack up losses on their portfolios, even during reasonably good times, as they continued to apply nineteenth-century standards and procedures to today's fast-moving markets. That has changed. Bank trust departments now move as quickly and aggressively in the markets as anybody else, and often their track records are as good as the best of the mutual funds. But who's got $500,000?

So the way for most investors to implement Plan B, then, is not to go to banks but to the huge American financial conglomerates—Merrill Lynch, Prudential-Bache, Shearson/American Express—which offer almost every shade and color of mutual fund you desire, and hire very capable people to manage them. So also the fund "family" groups, such as those managed by Value Line, or Kemper, or Oppenheimer. What they add up to is a situation where right here in the United States we investors have more good money managers at our disposal than are available in the rest of the world combined. Thus, as with electronics and genetic engineering, America seems also to enjoy a globally dominant position in the money management field.

But can you *really* depend upon the best of such managers to perform consistently? John Train, a New York investment counselor and columnist for *Forbes* magazine, in his excellent book *The Money Masters*, has demonstrated that the answer can be yes. He has tracked the lifetime records of nine such men who produced just such consistency of high performance. Two stand out: Warren Buffett and John Templeton. Both are loners. Buffett has stashed himself in Omaha, Nebraska, while Templeton goes about his self-appointed task of making money with money from the splendid isolation of Lyford Cay in the Bahamas.

How well have they done? "If you had put $10,000 in Mr. Buffett's original investment partnership at inception in 1956, you would have collected about $300,000 by the time he dissolved it at the end of 1969. He never had a down year," writes Train. How does Buffett do it? Essentially by buying the stocks of listed companies selling at substantial discounts from their book value and then being patient—waiting until the market price rises to the "correct" level, reflecting true book value, even if it takes *years*.

Today Mr. Buffett works via a publicly traded corporation, Berkshire Hathaway. Eighteen years ago, when Buffett took it over, the book value of that company was $19.46 a share. In 1983 it was up to $737.43 a share. A mutual fund, the Sequoia Fund, runs a parallel portfolio by more or less duplicating Buffett's every move. The performance of the Sequoia Fund between the end of 1972 and the beginning of 1982 was not bad either:

up 396.70 percent, ranking it ninth in terms of American mutual funds during that period of time. Consistency.

Let's look at John Templeton. His approach is to search among many markets for companies selling for the smallest fraction of their true worth. In that respect his approach does not vary essentially from Buffett's. Where Templeton is probably unique among American money managers, however, is that he looks *everywhere*, not just in the United States, for those bargains that nobody else has yet spotted, from London to Amsterdam to Hong Kong. A key to his success has also been patience. On average Mr. Templeton holds stocks he buys for four years before cashing in for the profit. The results, according to Train, are impressive: "Over the 20 years ending December 31, 1978, a $1,000 investment in his fund became worth $20,000." During the more recent ten-year period, ending December 31, 1982, the Templeton Fund (where anybody with $1,000 can participate) was up 216.83 percent.

So if and when you feel the time is right to play the market in general —when you sense that the rate of inflation is falling, or is low and promises to stay low, and when the prospects for overall economic growth are simultaneously good and improving—the first thing to do is to track down funds and fund managers with consistent high performance. Where? Go to the library. Ask for either the *Lipper Analytical Service* or the *Current Performance and Dividend Record* put out by the Wiesenberger Investment Service. If you prefer no-load funds (ones that do not charge a sales commission), the No-Load Fund Association in New York now provides comparative track records. When you've found your winner, you can only hope and trust that your fund manager will outperform the rising market as he adroitly moves from airlines and brokerage stocks to auto and retailing equities to issues related to energy and heavy industry, piling up capital gains for you in the process.

What has this got to do with our two scenarios? A lot. During the past couple of decades we have moved from good times to bad times and back to good times. Almost any fool can make money in a roaring bull market. But it takes a certain kind of genius to consistently make money during down markets as well as up markets. I have suggested that after mid-decade this current bull market is going to die. I do *not* see a Crash of '86 along Joe Granville lines, but I do see an end to the current investment honeymoon. After all, *all* honeymoons end. When *this* one does, you will be smart to have your money under the management of someone who has gone through this before and has proven that he or she can cope with it without losing *your* shirt. This approach requires patience, often a lot of it.

On the other hand, if my relative optimism proves misguided, and if in 1985 it becomes increasingly clear to you that the direly pessimistic scenario described earlier in this book is coming true, then I suggest you simply call your investment banker in San Francisco and your mutual fund manager in Chicago or New York and tell them to sell you out at market and wire you the proceeds. I say this despite the lock-up principle I recommended earlier where high-tech stocks are concerned, for that advice holds only for periods of moderate cyclical movements. But it is simply dumb to just sit there and ride out *really* bad years. We had one of those "bad" periods between mid-1981 and mid-1982, and, on average, the prices of high-tech stocks plummeted 50 percent! Who needs that?

Where to put the money when you get out of the market? Put it into a money market account at the bank. Your principal is safe there. Your income in the form of interest will be essentially indexed to the rate of inflation. Thus such an account will provide an ideal haven for your funds while the economic storm rages outside.

While your funds are "parked," plot the next *economic* scenario, and plan your next *investment* move accordingly.

Chapter 21

o◯oo◯oo◯o

Foreign Exchange

T HE FOREIGN-EXCHANGE MARKET is where the trends in economics, finance and politics come together. If you want to try to make money by guessing where the yen is going relative to the dollar during the next ninety days, or the mark relative to the pound sterling, you can trade these currencies either through your bank or through the commodity exchange in Chicago or New York.

My suggestion if you intend to do this as an individual: Don't!

Foreign-exchange trading is strictly for experts and full-time traders. If you stand an 85 percent chance of getting taken to the cleaners in cocoa or pork bellies, my guess is that where marks and yen and pesos are concerned the odds against you rise to 95 percent. But whether you speculate or not in foreign exchange, the fate of the dollar relative to sterling or the mark or the yen in the 1980's is an important parameter for the very reasons cited above: this is the market where everything comes together.

This is why I have always been fascinated with foreign exchange, and no doubt also why I tend to go on a bit when I discuss this market. If you choose to forgo my attempts to explain why currencies behave as they do, just skip the next few pages: subsequent to them, I finally get down to making concrete forecasts of future foreign-exchange trends. In recent years, every spring I have been invited to give a speech to the West Coast FOREX—the association of foreign exchange dealers—where I am expected to make my fearless forecasts concerning currency trends for the rest of the year. These evenings provide more fun than substance, since foreign-exchange dealers are a wonderful bunch—they all drink and smoke a lot, in pleasant contrast to the usual pseudo-Puritan crowds these days; they also cuss a lot, and know the world's very latest dirty jokes provided via telex by their counterparts in Tokyo, Frankfurt or Milan. They deal in tens of millions of dollars with one phone call, and that phone call is usually in fractured English, which is the lingua franca of the profession, even in Moscow. If they are wrong, they can drop tens of thousands of dollars in five minutes. Such risk-taking combined with the smoking and drinking takes its toll, of course. The result is that foreign-exchange dealers, like air traffic controllers, burn out early. They also heckle quite a bit during speeches, especially if what you said the prior year turned out to be dead wrong.

During the past couple of years the crowd has behaved reasonably well, since it has been difficult to be dead wrong provided one simply predicted a strong dollar. Why? Well, I have a theory, shared by the gurus of the Bank for International Settlements—that Swiss institution which is owned by the world's principal central banks—namely, that major currencies seem to get caught in either vicious or virtuous cycles, and once one of these processes starts, it tends to perpetuate itself not just for weeks or months but for years.

During the 1970's the U.S. dollar got caught in what appeared to be the vicious cycle to end all vicious cycles. As we have seen, during the Johnson years when we were supposed to produce guns and butter without any tax increases, the United States began to monetize its growing debt. As a result the stock of U.S. dollars floating around the world began to increase at a tremendous rate. With the dollar now becoming a surplus international "commodity," faith in that currency as a store of value began to fade. When Nixon simply closed the American gold window in 1971, meaning that foreign governments holding these stocks of excess dollars no longer had the option of cashing them in for American gold, such faith was lost absolutely.

Let's look at the trend, as measured by the dollar's performance relative to the German mark (the representative currency of the so-called hard currency bloc in the rest of the world) that resulted (Figure 23).

Why the nine-year down trend in the value of the dollar from 1970 to 1979? The trend in the price of a currency, relative to other currencies, is fundamentally a function of relative rates of inflation. For example, when the current rate of inflation in the United States was 5 percent but generally expected to rise above 10 percent (as in the mid-1970's) while at the same time the German rate of inflation was 5 percent but headed toward 3 percent, it was an absolutely *sure* thing that the dollar was going

FIGURE 23
The International Value of U.S. Dollars in Terms of German Marks

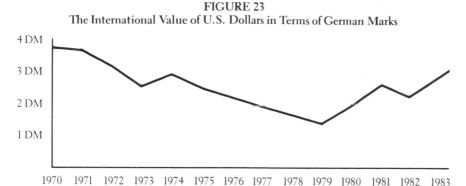

to trend down in value relative to the German mark in the ensuing years, as in fact it did. Or take France. In the first two years under Mitterrand France followed highly expansionistic "Keynesian" policies while the rest of Europe was run by ultraconservatives who were willing to undergo deep recession and high unemployment in order to get prices back under control. The resulting disparity between the continuing high French rate of inflation and the low and rapidly falling rates of inflation in the rest of the world led to enormous increases in French imports, as exports stagnated. Soon France had a trade deficit of $17 billion a year. With repeated devaluations inevitable, everybody who could got his money out of France. To counter the capital flight, the French central bank wasted over $10 billion "buying in" francs to hold the exchange rate. Such actions produced temporary recoveries, but of course they ultimately failed. After the third "Mitterrand" devaluation in early 1983 the French government had no choice but to give up its expansionistic policies, and introduce austerity and exchange controls. Eventually it worked. The capital flight reversed itself; the franc was stabilized . . . but only after it had sunk to a sixty-year low relative to the dollar.

Lesson: It does not pay to be the odd man out in monetary policy, as the United States found out in the 1970's, or in economic policy, as France learned in the 1980's. Paradoxically Mitterrand is now trying to talk the United States into returning to *fixed* exchange rates, since through some process of contorted Gallic reasoning he has concluded that it was floating rates that led to France's problems in the first place. If, in fact, in 1982–83 the world *had* been on a fixed exchange-rate system, France would probably have had to borrow an additional $10 billion or $15 billion on top of that $50 billion it already owed in order to defend the fixed franc/dollar parity to the death—no doubt with results just as futile as those achieved by their defense of the franc rate at successively lower levels under the floating system.

Today there is simply so much hot money floating around the world —a trillion dollars and more—that it is folly even to contemplate a return to fixed rates. Speculators could knock off any currencies they chose, probably one after the other, simply by overwhelming the central banks' defenses, and we would again lurch from one global currency crisis to the next. That's all we need on top of the latent banking crisis and the real deficit crisis. Right?

So much for basic trends: now, what about the fluctuations around them? Intervention by a central bank, such as France attempted, can temporarily turn things around. So if you are a short-term currency speculator, you should practice reading the minds of the people running the Bank of England or the Bundesbank in Germany. But in addition to intervention, in recent times fluctuations around a trend have been, for the most part, a function of interest rates. When in 1979–80 you could get 20 percent interest on ninety-day dollar deposits in London or New York, and only 8 percent on deutsche mark deposits in Frankfurt, if you were a multinational corporation with a huge cash float you probably opted for the dollar for ninety days instead of the mark, even though you were fully aware of the relative inflationary situations. Why? Because experience has shown that where *major* currencies are concerned, when the interest differential is way out of line by historical standards, it is usually worth taking the risk of "bucking the trend." (Conversely, where *minor* currencies are concerned, the risk is seldom worth it. You could, for example, often get 75 percent or even 125 percent per annum interest on Mexican pesos in 1982, but you would have lost your shirt in the process as the peso fell.)

But it was not interest rates alone that did, or could, finally brake the downward vicious cycle of the dollar and eventually turn it around. It was the realization in 1979 that the new man heading the Federal Reserve Board, Paul Volcker, knew what he was doing, and that he was going to break the back of inflation in the United States, if necessary through monetary policy alone. The money supply that had doubled over the previous eight years suddenly stopped growing. Thus Volcker produced a killer credit crunch and sky-high dollar interest rates. More important, this credit crunch resulted in the deepest U.S. recession since World War II. *That* really did the trick, for the recession was so severe that not only did it reduce inflation, it killed it, the rate falling from over 12 percent to zero in two years.

Thus it was first the profit motive—the attraction of the dollar interest rates—and then the attraction of the currency of a nation whose rate of inflation was falling to zero as a store of value that changed the global pattern of currency trends. The dollar rose 35 percent against the mark; 30 percent against the Swiss franc; 25 percent against the yen; 30 percent against sterling; 40 percent against the French franc; and although we know Mr. Nixon doesn't care, by the same amount against the lira.

So the 1970–78 vicious cycle during which the U.S. dollar fell from grace suddenly changed into the 1979–83 virtuous cycle and the dollar was once again king.

So much for the past. What about the next three or four years?

I think they will be divided into two distinct periods. Although the ascendancy of the dollar reached its high point in 1983, its strength will persist as long as very high nominal and real interest rates continue in the United States. That, in turn, seems guaranteed by the borrowing necessary to cover the $200 billion federal deficits, and the rise of private borrowing currently stimulated by the recovery. The combined loan demand simply will not allow a major further fall in interest rates. On the other hand, the large "residue" of unemployment continues to act as a substantial drag on resumption of cost-push inflation. So at least in 1984 inflation will remain low. Thus the gap between inflation and interest rates—real interest rates—will continue to be large; in fact, it will continue to be extraordinarily large not only by *historical* standards but, more important where foreign exchange is concerned, also by current *international* standards. The gap between inflation and interest rates in Germany, Switzerland and Japan, for instance, will remain in the 2 percent range. Here it will remain in the 4–5 percent range, ruling out, I would think, any collapse of the dollar in the immediate future.

Beyond that, things get much hazier. Paradoxically, one reason that the dollar has been strong is the fact that the United States has been running record budgetary deficits. We all know that in the *long* run such deficits are inflationary, but in the *short* run, as we have just seen, high public-sector credit demands are primarily responsible for keeping interest rates high, maintaining the international attractiveness of the dollar as a place to "park" funds. But as the "long run" starts to catch up with us and *if* an ever larger proportion of that debt is monetized, then the threat of inflation will return, and so will the risk of sticking with the dollar for short-term gain. The next turning point could be just around the corner: then the deficits that had been good for the dollar in 1983 will be devastating for it in 1986.

Many American economists and most government officials today feel that a substantially weaker dollar would, in fact, be a good thing. The strong dollar which has prevailed since 1979 has made our products costly for the rest of the world, and imports cheap. The unemployment that resulted in American export-oriented industries, or in those industries especially exposed to foreign competition in the home market, no doubt contributed to the severity of the recent recession. At the same time, a much weaker dollar—by raising the cost of imports—would tend to accelerate the return of inflation to the American scene, something that might well start to happen soon even without any help from that particular quarter.

To be sure, however, talking about the advantages of a weaker dollar and actually getting one's way are two very different things these days. We would like to reduce our unemployment by increasing our exports. But so would the Germans . . . and the British and the Dutch and the Danes. A "weak" mark protects the competitive position of Germany's export industries and also protects the German home market from imports.

The danger is that without such protection in the form of "undervalued" currencies, then the temptation to protect one's own through other methods will become increasingly attractive to politicians of whatever nationality. In other words, a return to the type of overt trade protectionism that was so prevalent in the 1930's.

This was, in fact, a choice that France faced in 1983. Because France has a habit of going its own way and letting the rest of the world be damned, many investors feared that it would revert to the tactics of the 1930's. During that decade not only France but everybody else, led unfortunately by the United States, sought to protect domestic industries and the people they employed from foreign competition through tariffs and import quotas. As we know, in the end everybody suffered, since the result was a collapse in international trade. The *global* level of economic activity was reduced so much that the *national* employment situations went from bad to much worse in every country without exception. It is almost impossible to find an economist alive today who would advocate a return to such suicidal policies . . . except in England, and more specifically at Cambridge.

The Cambridge economists use Britain as their model, but I think the recent case of France makes the point more realistically. As we have seen, in the 1981–83 period France got out of step with the rest of the world when it followed expansionistic fiscal and monetary policies designed to increase aggregate demand in order to spur economic growth and so reduce domestic unemployment. What happened instead was that though demand rose, instead of being directed at *French* products, it "leaked" massively across the borders and was directed at *German* cars, *Italian* textiles and *Japanese* electronics. The Cambridge school suggests that if France erected import barriers, such leakage would stop and the French economy would prosper (just as Mitterrand had intended). According to this theory, it would prosper to such a degree that not only would full employment be restored in France but in the end, barriers or not, the volume of France's international trade would end up greater than ever before, as would ultimately the world's and everybody would live happily ever after.

Their prescription for Britain (one equally applicable to Belgium, France and, perhaps some day, the United States) was stated bluntly in the *Cambridge Journal of Economics:* "Fiscal expansion accompanied by direct control of imports (whether through tariffs or quotas) is the only practical means by which the U.K., and probably several other industrialized countries, can sustain expansion of national output sufficient to restore full employment in our decade."

But won't that just perpetuate, even accentuate, obsolescence in Britain or wherever else such policies are attempted? No, they claim. "Control of imports need not 'featherbed' inefficiency in domestic industries. On the contrary, expansion of demand made possible by import control is likely to assist innovation and productivity growth."

There are plenty of critics of this theory, but a question these critics must ask is whether Japan has not in fact been practicing just these policies during the past two decades, and with tremendous success.

I'm afraid that if high structural unemployment continues during this decade, the temptation for politicians, especially in Europe, to try a "new" approach, along the Cambridge lines, is going to grow. Should the continent swing leftward again, radical governments might very well sacrifice free trade for full employment. The strong American welcome to suggestions for legislation requiring very high local content for any foreign cars sold in the United States suggests a growing tendency here too for such ideas. But for the period we are here concerned with—the next three or four years—I think that the danger of protectionism will remain latent rather than real. Nations will adjust to shifts in their international competitive position chiefly through foreign exchange and adaptations of domestic fiscal and monetary policies to currently prevalent world "standards."

Which brings us back to square one: Whither the world's chief currencies in the mid-1980's? For those who would like to speculate in them despite all my warnings, I have the following thoughts:

1. Hard-currency areas are going to remain hard-currency areas. Thus Germany and its monetary satellites—Holland and Austria and to a lesser degree Denmark—will inevitably continue to give the highest priority to price stability, even in the face of unprecedentedly high structural unemployment. The powers-that-be in this region are firmly convinced that inflation will *not* cure unemployment, and probably only exacerbates it in the long run. The men who run Switzerland (yes, it's still only the men) share this philosophy. Furthermore, since Germany is Switzerland's dominant trading partner, the first priority of the Swiss National Bank is to ensure that its franc and the German mark move in tandem; a stable Swiss franc/mark relationship is the goal; what happens to the franc/dollar relationship is today of secondary importance. Thus as the German mark goes so will go the Swiss franc.

With rates of inflation near zero in Central Europe, and likely to stay extraordinarily low in the foreseeable future, there are hardly any grounds now to expect future dollar appreciation relative to these "hard" currencies. Thus one can reasonably assume that the dollar's five-year honeymoon in Central Europe is over—its virtuous cycle has ended. If the pessimistic scenario proves correct, and America attempts to reflate, a vicious cycle will probably start again where the dollar is concerned, since *fundamentally* Central Europe is more committed than the United States to low rates of inflation *at any cost.*

2. Losers will remain losers. Chief among these will continue to be the United Kingdom and the pound sterling. In 1983 the Manchester *Guardian* asked "What happens when the oil runs out?" What happens is this: the British government's revenue from North Sea oil production today is around 10 billion pounds annually ($25 billion), representing 500 pounds per British taxpayer (which is one reason, as I have already said, why U.K. budgetary deficits are so low by current international standards). Starting in 1986 such revenue will fall by one billion pounds a year. Unless this loss is compensated for by a reindustrialization process, the accompanying decline of oil exports will turn the U.K.'s trade balance sharply negative. The result will be another collapse of sterling unless the government then undertakes yet another round of deflation and pushes the U.K. economy

into yet another steep decline. But this will mean 15 or 16 percent rates of unemployment, which seem unacceptable.

The alternative is for Britain to try to halt and even reverse the deindustrialization which has been going on for decades but has accelerated of late (since 1979 manufacturing output in the U.K. has dropped another 20 percent), a process which has been temporarily "masked" by the North Sea oil boom. The odds are that Britain in 1985 or 1986 may have to try what France did in 1981 and 1982—to reflate domestic demand. If Britain does not go the "Cambridge school" route of protectionism, this reflation, the *Guardian* points out, "could lead to trade deficits, continued falls in sterling, and financial crisis even before the oil starts to run out."

You see what I mean? Sterling will decline in either case.

3. If you applied purchasing power parity to the Japanese yen, that is, if you calculated how many yen it would take to buy a typical "basket" of goods that costs $100 in the United States, the yen would probably be 20 percent higher in value than it is today. Normally such currency parities are reached over a period of years through "natural" market forces under conditions of free trade. But in the case of Japan such forces have always been inhibited by governmental policies. Japan's market for foreign goods is *still* tiny, since imports are almost totally discouraged by myriad restrictions and barriers. Japan's capital market is so controlled that the yen remains relatively unattractive to foreign investors, meaning that its "price" is not being bid up due to a steady accumulation of yen by nonresidents (as has been the case for years with the U.S. dollar). The relative unattractiveness of the yen has been accentuated by the fact that interest rates in Japan are consistently kept well below the rates on the dollar, or even on most European currencies.

The resulting undervaluation of the yen gives Japan, in essence, a 20 percent price advantage in export markets. Since Japan's import restrictions guarantee that this undervalued yen will not lead to massive imports, the Japanese have it both ways.

Will that change? Probably some, but not much. It is the United States that has been pushing Japan hard, sometimes very hard indeed, to remove those import restrictions. But there is a growing school of thought in Washington that feels that this does not make sense. For even *if* we succeeded, the probable beneficiaries would be not *us*, but all the *rest* of the world's low-cost or high-quality exporters, ranging from Korea to Hong Kong to Singapore, where the low-cost advantage would pay off in

Japan; or West Germany or Switzerland or Sweden, where high-quality products are concerned. The Japanese would buy Mercedeses, not Chevrolets; they would import steel from Korea, not steel produced by Bethlehem in Pittsburgh. Therefore, why should the United States further risk its political/military alliance with Japan by pushing trade policy changes which will help the United States very little?

This school contends that what the United States *should* press the Japanese government for is to encourage and facilitate *capital* exports from Japan. Japan has the highest rate of savings on earth, giving it what by international standards amounts to a large "exportable surplus." If $20 billion or $30 billion of such savings flowed to the United States each year, it would ease our latent "credit crunch" problem. The drawback of such an opening-up of the Japanese money and capital markets to foreign borrowers is that as Japanese capital moved into the dollar, attracted by much higher interest rates in New York, it would push its exchange value even higher, or seen from the other side, exert *further* downward pressure on the yen, thus contributing to, not reversing, the yen's undervaluation. So although on the surface this idea appears to be a great one, once everybody thinks it through I suspect it will be quietly forgotten.

The interim solution will come from intervention by the Japanese Central Bank . . . its *selling* of dollars, its "buying in" of yen. As a result, on balance I would think that the yen will correct by 10 percent, to the 210 yen to the dollar range, but not more. The ultimate solution will have to come in the form of Japan abolishing its equivalent of Regulation Q. If banks in Tokyo were free to compete for deposits, as banks now are in the United States, yen interest rates would no doubt rise to "international" levels, attracting investors worldwide and bringing the international value of the yen up to a level more realistically in line with other currencies.

4. Of course future exchange rates are fundamentally affected by what happens in the U.K., Germany and Japan, but they are inevitably even more affected by what the Big Brother in these relationships is doing, or not doing, at home. I think it fair to say that should the current low-inflationary recovery in the United States keep on going, and if a Republican Administration is returned to office in 1984, that Administration—like the governments of Central Europe—will continue to give highest priority to maintaining low rates of inflation. Under such circumstances, the chances are excellent that, in contrast to the last decade and a half, we shall see the dollar in neither a vicious nor a virtuous cycle relative to

the rest of the world's chief currencies, but rather we shall see relatively *stable* rates emerging, with the exception of the pound sterling. The mark, the Swiss franc and the yen will all gain. But compared to the 1970's, the 1980's will be a decade of relative calm where currencies are concerned.

However, should this current economic recovery falter prematurely, and falter badly, accompanied first by a credit crunch, then an attempt at reflation and then a return to zero growth, double-digit inflation and a prime once again at 15 percent—in other words, our pessimistic scenario—I think it fair to say that by mid-decade the dollar will once again find itself in a downward cycle, probably not as severe as in the 1970's, because nominal interest rates in the United States at the beginning of this new cycle would this time be not only positive but very positive, enticing people to hold dollars for short-term gain, even though inflation was once again undermining the currency as a store of value.

The return of the Democrats to the White House in 1985 will tend to accelerate and exacerbate the deterioration of the dollar, since it is widely held among bankers and foreign-exchange dealers that by shifting priorities from fighting inflation to promoting employment, the Democrats would do to the dollar in mid-decade what Mitterrand did to the French franc at the beginning of the 1980's. Under the Democrats, both government spending and taxation would begin to skyrocket once again. Soon so would the rate of inflation. The "benign" years of the Reagan interlude (from their point of view) would already have ended. Therefore they would start dumping the dollar.

It is not a nice world.

Chapter 22

∘◯∘∘◯∘∘◯∘

Conclusion

NOT ONLY IS IT not a nice world, it is a world once again in rapid transition. For it is now apparent that the 1980's represent an interregnum during which the classic industries of the original capitalistic world, meaning Western Europe, the United States and Canada, are going to shrink dramatically. Automobiles, shipbuilding, steel and all the other heavy-machinery, metal-bending, metal-using industries are beginning to wind down as primary "wealth-creators" in our society. Taking their place, and eliminating the jobs of the blue-collar workers who have traditionally toiled in such industries in the West, are going to be steel mills and assembly-line workers in Korea and Taiwan and Brazil and ultimately Nigeria and Pakistan.

America's energy-intensive, raw materials–intensive, labor-intensive industries can no longer compete even in their home markets. With an automobile or steel worker costing $50,000 a year; with energy at ten times the price it was when many of these industries built their facilities; and with the raw materials base in America extensively depleted, this should hardly come as a surprise. What is surprising is only that it came this late. The result, as we all know, is that immense pockets of *permanently* idle plant and equipment and of unwillingly unemployed are accumulating not only in the upper Midwest of the United States, but also in the Ruhr of West Germany, in the coal and steel communities of Belgium and France, in the Midlands of England, in the eastern provinces of Canada.

So unemployment is the basic problem facing our system today.

Parallel to this fundamental shift in the *real* economy, the 1980's has seen the rise of two fundamental problems in the *money* economy: the buildup of immense *debts* in the Third World and Eastern Europe which cannot be repaid, and immense *structural,* that is, built in, deficits in the West which cannot be eliminated. Both situations require continual massive borrowings lest the world face an unprecedented economic/social crisis. If we do not lend Mexico more and more, the result, ultimately, will be revolution south of the American border. This we cannot allow to happen. Period. If we do not maintain our own system of entitlements and social services which must be financed by massive borrowings, especially in the face of vast structural unemployment—the result, ultimately, will be "revolution" in Oakland and Detroit and Miami. That we certainly cannot allow to happen. Nor can the United States suddenly, massively and unilaterally cut its defense spending. That would amount to nothing short of an invitation to the Soviet Union to cause trouble wherever and whenever it could—especially in the Third World, specifically in Latin America—which could end up being even *more* expensive for the United States and the West in the long run than spending hundreds of billions *now* on our military deterrent.

All this, the pessimists say, raises the question: Where is all the money going to come from?

Governments are going to have to borrow more than $600 billion each year; annual net personal savings which feed the capital markets of the West with fresh money will be only in the $500 billion range. Paradoxically, according to the pessimists, the stronger this current recovery turns out to be, the more acute the danger that we are heading toward another credit crunch as rising private-sector financing requirements collide with unprecedentedly high governmental financing needs.

Result, they say: soaring interest rates after mid-decade which must be reversed lest they immediately dump the economies of the West back into recession. Reaction: the governments and central banks of the West, led by the United States, will reflate. Ultimately the Federal Reserve Board will *have* to take the pressures off the capital markets by increasingly monetizing the deficits. But this attempt, like all similar attempts in the past, will abort, the cynics say. As inflationary expectations rise, so will interest rates after only a brief pause, and what we will end up with in 1986–87 is another recession, accompanied by inflation approaching double digits and interest rates even higher with unemployment this time headed toward 12–13 percent in the United States.

It will be only a matter of time, the pessimists claim, before this renewed stagflation again spreads through the West. When the engine of economic recovery, the United States, falters, Western Europe, which in the 1980's is much more vulnerable to economic shock than at any time since World War II because deindustrialization on that continent has reached a more advanced stage, will soon suffer from the same malaise but in a more severe form. *Der Spiegel,* the West German equivalent of *Time* magazine, which occasionally commissions in-depth analyses of economic problems, in a recent study concluded that even *without* another major economic downturn, unemployment in Germany will rise to between 13 and 14 percent by the end of the 1980's. For Germany is really just one great big factory, engaged predominantly in the production and export of those "classic" manufactures of the Industrial Revolution: steel, automobiles, chemicals, ships . . . all of which are on their way out. German development of high-tech industries has seriously lagged behind that of the United States and Japan. As unbelievable as this may sound, German universities have ignored the computer, a "machine" which Germans feel has no serious role to play in the teaching of traditional academic disciplines. This does not bode well for the continent as a whole, for Germany is to Europe what the United States is to the world. If the United States falters once again, Germany will falter even worse—lacking new industries able to pick up the slack—and ensure that Europe's unemployment will reach levels—25 million people—that just a few years ago would have been considered unthinkable.

Even a majority of pessimists, however, do *not* conclude that this is the end of the West as we have come to know and love it. Along with the optimists, they feel that there *is* a solution, in fact a single solution to all three major problems facing us in the 1980's—unemployment, huge structural fiscal deficits and the debt overhang in the Third World— namely the resumption of sustained economic growth in the West.

They would tend to agree with the optimists that such growth will come mainly from two processes: through the wealth-creating application of high technology to almost every activity our society is engaged in, and the accompanying buildup of the service support industries which this high-tech society will both demand and be able to afford.

Where the two schools disagree is on timing. The pessimists feel that our future has not yet begun; that the 1980's are an *inter*regnum; that it will be the 1990's and beyond that will provide the new economic "order." The optimists feel that these processes are well under way, and that the economies of the West will continue to grow, becoming increasingly healthy, in fact *so* healthy that fears of a serious relapse in this decade are unrealistic.

Let's reexamine the case the optimists put forward. I call it the 4-5-3 school of thought because its adherents expect 4 percent real growth, a 5 percent prime rate of interest and 3 percent inflation to be the norm as the 1980's progresses, and then extend indefinitely into the future. Their case for growth rests to a substantial degree on the assumption that the decade of oil shocks is over; that in contrast to the 1970's, when growth was twice stopped dead by massive increases in the world oil price, with OPEC now lamed if not dead, the oil shock of the 1980's is going to be in the form of highly *positive* impulses as periodic decreases in energy costs occur. Rather than considering the currently high budgetary deficits as potentially destructive, they consider them "Keynesian," at least in the short run: that these massive deficits contribute to overall aggregate demand in a major fashion, exerting a positive effect on recovery perhaps as important as decreasing energy costs. The deep recession of 1981–82 cried out for a massive dose of Keynesianism, and that, paradoxically, is precisely what the Reagan Administration has inadvertently supplied.

The *structural* unemployment problem, which cannot be solved by demand stimulus, *is* serious, they recognize, and unfortunately can only be alleviated gradually. But the situation is by no means hopeless. Look at the farm sector in the United States, they remind us. One hundred years ago half of all Americans worked there. If you had said *then* that by 1984 only 3 percent of the American labor force could find work on the farm, you would have been told that this was flat-out impossible. So it is today with the so-called classical industries. They are being phased out, but in an orderly fashion, and not in a straight-line, straight-down process. The United States is going to have some good, even excellent, years in the 1980's for the automotive industry; ditto for what remains of the farm equipment industry and even certain sectors of the steel industry. When the pent-up demand for housing is unleashed by falling interest rates, the biggest industry of all, construction, could boom as seldom before. So the growth potential, and the impulses that will lead to a realization of that potential, are here, and they are here *now*.

Furthermore, the optimists claim, there is no reason why this recovery must be aborted by either a credit crunch or a return to high rates of inflation, or both. Regarding the credit markets, as the economy grows in strength, so will tax receipts. In the out-years where it will *count*, namely after mid-decade, such increased receipts will reduce federal deficits by half and relieve the pressure from that quarter that might otherwise have led to a credit crunch and higher interest rates, as the private sector continues to expand. Not only that, but in this 4-5-3 situation private savings are *bound* to increase, aided in no small measure by the lower tax rates introduced by the Reagan Administration, and the fact that each and every taxpayer can and increasingly will sock away $2,000 in new savings each year in his IRA account, and as much as $30,000 a year in tax-free Keogh plans where the doctors and dentists and lawyers are concerned. So the pessimists' equation is wrong: you won't see borrowing needs vastly exceeding new savings in 1986 or 1987. If anything, there could well be a savings surplus, ensuring the continuation of a decade-long down trend in interest rates which began in 1982.

As for a collapse of the world banking system arising out of Third World debts, it just won't happen, the optimists claim. No government on earth could afford to allow even *one* major international bank to go broke. Therefore they will simply finance and refinance the debtor countries, either directly or through the IMF and the BIS, thus providing insurance against any massive defaults. There can be no doubt that this will happen, for the alternative is financial suicide by the West, where the system will go up in smoke in a final violent explosion, just as Karl Marx predicted it would eventually have to do.

As for the feared revival of inflation, it is nonsense, the optimists say. We are in better shape now than we have ever been since the 1950's. "Do you *really* believe that inflation can revive soon when ten million people are out of work?" they ask. "Do you *really* believe inflation is a danger when only 80 percent of plant and equipment is being utilized?" What is going to push up wages under these conditions? Where are the "bottlenecks" going to appear?

Nor is there any danger that we will "import" inflation from abroad. From Canada to England to Germany to France there is the same labor "overhang" and the same excess capacity "overhang." With the dollar likely to remain strong, this eliminates even further the chances that the United States will import inflation and then reexport it later on. So in the "real" economy, the chances that cost-push inflation will revive in this decade seem very remote indeed.

One must reach the same conclusion, they say, when one assesses the future by considering only the so-called money economy. With savings climbing, with government deficits declining after mid-decade, precluding any credit-crunch danger, there will be absolutely no need to crank up the money supply. In fact, as it becomes apparent that our future is 4 percent growth, 5 percent interest rates and 3 percent inflation, and especially as inflationary expectations subside, the need for the Fed to "nurse" money and capital markets will likewise abate. The M1 watchers on Wall Street will have to find a new profession. Money supply increases will again match real economic growth—that 4 percent per annum—and money, per se, will again assume a subordinate role in our economic world. It will become neutral, a means of exchange and a store of value.

So who's going to be right?

I like some of the reasoning on *both* sides. The optimists are convincing on inflation: there seems to me to be no chance of a *runaway* inflation in this decade. But I certainly can't buy their 4-5-3 theory. Just as the economic gurus of the 1970's were dead wrong in assuming that the trees of inflation were going to grow into the heavens, so also, I suspect, those who now see a decade of uninterrupted growth are likewise being carried away by the moment. We are no more able to "fine-tune" the business cycle out of existence in the 1980's than we were in the 1960's. Therefore I do not believe that worldwide government deficits are going to be easily financed or reduced. Savings may indeed increase. But against the background of the savings rate in the United States dropping to a thirty-three-year low in 1983, it hardly seems likely that they will recover quickly enough and sufficiently to eliminate the possibility, or even probability, of a major credit crunch after mid-decade, one that we will try to escape by inflationary monetary policies. In other words, I do not believe we can go through a period of severe structural changes in our economy as smoothly as the optimists would have us believe. We will have relapses, perhaps even a serious relapse in this decade. There are more recessions in our future, and I would be surprised if we didn't get hit again, and hit hard, within three or four years. But I agree with the optimists where the Third World bank debt is concerned: we can't afford default, therefore it won't happen. But the price for that is to put the Third World on the dole, which will add yet another burden to an already overloaded public sector. Nevertheless, I think that, on balance, the 1980's are going to be a definite improvement over the roller-coaster of the 1970's—one that *almost* ended in a crash.

How to make money in the 1980's out of all this? It will require agility. For in contrast to the 1970's, we are not faced with a stark either/or choice—*either* invest in "real" assets *or* in "financial" assets—with the inherent danger that if you make that one wrong initial decision it will mean for the rest of the decade that you will either make nothing or lose your shirt. At the beginning of the 1970's if you made such a critical decision in principle and chose financial assets and stuck with them, what you probably made in the stock market was exactly *nothing*, while in the fixed-interest securities market, especially the municipal bond market, you got *killed* as interest rates rose to unprecedented levels, dropping the value of bonds by 50 percent or more. If there *was* a place to *make* money in the seventies, it was in *real* assets, as everybody who owned real estate found out, although in most cases not because they were smart but merely because they happened to have bought a house to live in. The small minority who made a deliberate, calculated decision to find inflation hedges in such real assets as gold and silver were among the select few who made out like bandits.

The *financial* markets of the 1980's are not going to be dominated by a basic single *economic* phenomenon as the financial markets of the 1970's were by stagflation. We are going to see constant shifts in the contours of the economic landscape which will require basic shifts in what we do with our money. It is going to be a "now this, then that" sort of thing. "Now" stocks in general; "now" *and* "then" high-tech stocks in particular. "Now" municipal bonds and bond funds; "now" *and* "then" the insured, indexed-to-inflation money market accounts at banks. "Now" commercial real estate; "then," maybe, single-family houses. "Now" the dollar; "then" the Swiss franc, German mark and Japanese yen and maybe gold and maybe even silver. But *neither* "now" *nor* "then": the pound sterling, commodities.

I have strongly suggested that for day-to-day, week-to-week, even month-to-month management of your money you should turn it over to professionals. Where *you* have to make the decision is where year-to-year strategy is concerned. The management of your bond fund, for example, is *never* going to suggest that interest rates are about to take off and then advise you to get out of bonds and stay out for the next couple of years. *That* decision is going to have to be *yours*. And making such right decisions *in principle* and *in time* is going to be the key to successful investment in the 1980's. That is something you can do as well as anybody, and perhaps better. For there is literally *nobody* who is right all the time where investment strategy is concerned, and even most of the so-called experts inevitably let their egos get in the way of common sense, with predictable results. Have you, for instance, ever heard of a *really* rich economist?

My suggestion, therefore: read the financial section of your newspaper, subscribe to the *Wall Street Journal*, scan *Business Week* and *Fortune*, and then plot your own ideas regarding the future path of our *economy* in terms of the four key variables: real growth, money supply, inflation, interest rates. Then, from that, develop your own *money* guide for the future. If common sense tells you that the direction of the economy seems about to change, review your investment portfolio and then actually *do* something about it.

In the process you will find out that making money with money can be the greatest hobby there is. The money game is probably the most interesting and intellectually challenging sport that mankind has yet invented. But it is definitely not a spectator sport. It is also no longer a sport of kings. It is open to everybody with a few thousand dollars. So *play* it and *enjoy* it.

NOTES

PAGE

14   Professor Samuelson told us in his textbook: Paul A. Samuelson, *Economics*, 11th ed. (New York: McGraw-Hill, 1980).

16   cyclical behavior: Alfred L. Malabre, Jr., an editor of the *Wall Street Journal*, has written an excellent book on this subject—*Investing for Profit in the Eighties: The Business Cycle System* (New York: Doubleday, 1982).

20   "a contagion of fear . . .": Theodore H. White, *America in Search of Itself: The Making of the President 1956–1980* (New York: Harper & Row, 1982), p. 158.

23   "What will rates do now? . . .": Peter Brimelow, "Talking Money with Milton Friedman," *Barron's*, October 25, 1982, p. 7.

24   "the belief is now widely held . . .": Bank for International Settlements, *Fifty-second Annual Report*, June 14, 1982, p. 47.

24   "In the longer run . . .": Ibid.

52   as Ezra Solomon . . . points out: Ezra Solomon, *Beyond the Turning Point: The U.S. Economy in the 1980s* (San Francisco: Freeman, 1982).

56   "The chances of getting stable monetary policy . . .": "Kudlow Attacks Stimulative Policy Idea to Curb Deficits," *Wall Street Journal*, December 8, 1982, p. 3.

57   "By 1988 . . .": Paul Blustein, "Feldstein Says Economic Growth Alone Won't Cut U.S. Deficit to Acceptable Level," *Wall Street Journal*, November 9, 1983, p. 4.

61   "To put the matter bluntly . . .": Peter G. Peterson, "Social Security: The Coming Crash," *New York Review of Books*, December 2, 1982, p. 34.

62   "The only alternative . . .": Ibid.

PAGE

66   "Experience unfortunately shows . . .": from *Le Monde*, June 18, 1983; quoted in "What Weapons Against War?," Manchester *Guardian*, July 3, 1983, p. 12.

73   "an accomplished horseman . . .": Art Pine, "IMF Turning the Table on Banks," *Wall Street Journal*, January 25, 1983, p. 37.

74   "To see why . . .": Walter B. Wriston, "Banking Against Disaster," New York *Times*, September 14, 1982, op-ed page.

76   "a 19th Century kind of financial panic . . .": Richard F. Janssen and Richard J. Levine, "A Threat to Economy Was Factor in Pressing U.S. to Defend Dollar," *Wall Street Journal*, November 6, 1978, p. 1.

76   "contingency plans for coping . . .": Hearings before a Subcommittee of the Committee on Government Operations, House of Representatives, Ninety-sixth Congress, First Session, July 16, 17, 18 and 26, 1979, "The Operations of Federal Agencies in Monitoring, Reporting on and Analyzing Foreign Investments in the United States" (Part 2—"OPEC Investment in the United States"), p. 117.

78   "We are on the way to hell . . .": David Brand, "In Western Europe Some Countries Owe Big Sums to Foreigners," *Wall Street Journal*, December 14, 1982, p. 118.

80   "bankers who did not go along . . .": H. Erich Heineman, "A Fed Push on Foreign Loans Seen," New York *Times*, January 14, 1983, p. 19.

94   "There is hope . . .": "Now Thrive Popeye," *The Economist*, January 29, 1983, p. 11.

98   forecast by Edward Jay Epstein in his book: Edward Jay Epstein, *The Rise and Fall of Diamonds: The Shattering of a Brilliant Illusion* (New York: Simon & Schuster, 1982).

98   "raising real growth . . .": Thomas O'Donnell, "The Strategy of Gloom," *Forbes*, January 31, 1983, p. 25.

99   "most discussions of the crowding out . . .": Evan G. Galbraith, "Private Borrowing and the Federal Deficit," *Wall Street Journal*, February 3, 1983, op-ed page.

100   "why we haven't seen the effect . . .": Ibid.

100   Hugo Uyterhoeven . . . has a better theory: Hugo Uyterhoeven, "So You Think Reaganomics Is Dead," *Wall Street Journal*, February 4, 1983, op-ed page.

102   "ridiculously high": Ibid.

127   "Whoops is a 'municipal corporation . . .' ": Norman W. Shainmark, Letters to the Editor, *Wall Street Journal*, June 27, 1983, p. 29.

127   "The electric-utility industry . . .": Geraldine Brooks, Ron Winslow and Bill Richards, "Utilities Face a Crisis over Nuclear Plants: Costs, Delays Mount," *Wall Street Journal*, December 1, 1983, p. 1.

PAGE

127   "Nobody ever thought . . .": Ibid.

128   "Nuclear plants are being built . . .": Ibid.

134   "it is quite possible . . .": *The Aden Analysis,* Vol. 2, No. iv, April 10, 1983, p. 3.

136   an analysis done by Dr. Horace W. Brock: Horace W. Brock, *The Future World Price of Gold* (Johannesburg, South Africa: Anglo American Corporation of South Africa, Ltd., 1981).

138   The *Wall Street Journal* tracked the anxiety "effect": information is from Roger Lowenstein, "Bad News Has Little Effect on Gold's Price," *Wall Street Journal,* January 21, 1981, and from a report in the *Wall Street Journal,* September 2, 1983.

143   Timothy Green, whose book: *The New World of Gold* (New York: Walker, 1982).

145   "That one statement . . .": Stanley W. Angrist, "Can Silver Shine Again?," *Forbes,* April 11, 1983, p. 208.

156   written by Robert Bruss: *The Smart Investor's Guide to Real Estate: Big Profits from Small Investors* (New York: Crown, 1981).

158   Beverly Tanner: *Shelter What You Make—Minimize the Take* (San Francisco: Harbor Publications, 1982).

169   an excellent book: Albert Toney and Thomas Tilling, *High Tech: How to Find and Profit from Today's New Super Stocks* (New York: Simon & Schuster, 1983).

170   "If you had put $10,000 . . .": John Train, *The Money Masters: Nine Great Investors, Their Winning Strategies and How You Can Apply Them* (New York: Harper & Row, 1980), p. 1.

171   "Over the 20 years . . .": Ibid, p. 160.

179   "Fiscal expansion . . .": Francis Cripps and Wynne Godley, "Control of Imports as a Means to Full Employment and the Expansion of World Trade: The U.K.'s Case," *Cambridge Journal of Economics,* Vol. 2, No. 3, September 1978, p. 327.

179   "Control of imports . . .": Ibid.

180   "What happens when the oil runs out?": title of an article by Francis Cripps and Wynne Godley, Manchester *Guardian,* May 27, 1983, p. 4.

181   "could lead to trade deficits . . .": Ibid.

INDEX

ABOUT THE AUTHOR

PAUL ERDMAN is the author of four best-selling novels, *The Billion Dollar Sure Thing, The Silver Bears, The Crash of '79,* and *The Last Days of America.* He is also an economist and international banker who received his Ph.D. summa cum laude from the University of Basel. He lectures widely before business audiences and has a popular weekly radio call-in show, "Money Talk," on KGO in San Francisco. He lives with his wife near Santa Rosa, California.